Presence-Centered Youth Ministry

GUIDING STUDENTS INTO SPIRITUAL FORMATION

Mike King

IVP Books

An imprint of InterVarsity Press
Downers Grove, Illinois

InterVarsity Press
P.O. Box 1400, Downers Grove, IL 60515-1426
World Wide Web: www.ivpress.com
E-mail: mail@ivpress.com

InterVarsity Press® is the book-publishing division of InterVarsity Christian Fellowship/USA®, a student movement active on campus at hundreds of universities, colleges and schools of nursing in the United States of America, and a member movement of the International Fellowship of Evangelical Students. For information about local and regional activities, write Public Relations Dept., InterVarsity Christian Fellowship/USA, 6400 Schroeder Rd., P.O. Box 7895, Madison, WI 53707-7895, or visit the IVCF website at <www.intervarsity.org>.

Scripture quotations, unless otherwise noted, are from the New Revised Standard Version of the Bible, copyright 1989 by the Division of Christian Education of the National Council of the Churches of Christ in the USA. Used by permission. All rights reserved.

"Conclusion: Where Are You Staying?" reprinted courtesy of Zondervan. Originally written for Tony Jones, The Sacred Way: Spiritual Practices for Everyday Life (Grand Rapids: Zondervan, 2004).

Design: Cindy Kiple

Images: Jesus: Scala/Art Resource, NY
        Teens against wall: Stockbyte/Getty Images

ISBN-10: 0-8308-3383-8
ISBN-13: 978-0-8308-3383-2

Printed in the United States of America ∞

Library of Congress Cataloging-in-Publication Data

King, Mike, 1957-
  Presence-centered youth ministry: guiding students into spiritual formation / Mike King.
        p. cm.
  Includes bibliographical references.
  ISBN-13: 978-0-8308-3383-2 (pbk.: alk. paper)
  ISBN-10: 0-8308-3383-8 (pbk.: alk. paper)
  1. Church work with youth. 2. Youth—Religious aspects.
3. Spiritual formation. I. Title.
  BV4447.K56 2006
  259'.23—dc22

                                                                    2006020862

| P | 19 | 18 | 17 | 16 | 15 | 14 | 13 | 12 | 11 | 10 | 9 | 8 | 7 | 6 | 5 | 4 | 3 | 2 | 1 |
| Y | 21 | 20 | 19 | 18 | 17 | 16 | 15 | 14 | 13 | 12 | 11 | 10 | 09 | 08 | 07 | 06 |

"Make no mistake: *Presence-Centered Youth Ministry* is about God's presence, not ours—which right away puts Mike King's approach to youth ministry in a class of its own. King transcends 'liberal/conservative' stereotypes by putting ancient spiritual practices at the heart of our ministry with young people—practices that center us in the presence of God. If you're not won by the teenagers you meet in these pages, you'll be won by the glimpses of how King's own ministry helps youth 'practice the presence of God.' If Brother Lawrence had been a youth pastor, this book would have been his favorite resource."

KENDA CREASY DEAN, PARENT, PASTOR, ASSOCIATE PROFESSOR OF YOUTH, CHURCH AND CULTURE, PRINCETON THEOLOGICAL SEMINARY, AND AUTHOR OF *PRACTICING PASSION: YOUTH AND THE QUEST FOR A PASSIONATE CHURCH*

"With *Presence-Centered Youth Ministry*, Mike King has given us a road map to the tectonic shift underway in student ministry. At turns personal, challenging, testimonial and prophetic, this book will surely capture the hearts of many youth workers. Mike speaks from experience, yet with humility, and he is truly setting the course for a new day in youth ministry."

TONY JONES, NATIONAL COORDINATOR OF EMERGENT-U.S. (www.emergentvillage.com), AND EDITOR OF *YOU CONVERTED ME: THE CONFESSIONS OF ST. AUGUSTINE*

"Mike King has started a conversation that's long overdue and frequently ignored in youth ministry circles. In this thoughtful book he tells his own story with humble vulnerability, exposes the sacred cows we've let graze for far too long on the youth ministry landscape, and helps us see that ministry isn't about facilitating and teaching outward behavorial conformity. I'm sure this book will make many uncomfortable because of its subject and recommendations. Pick it up. Don't put it down. Prayerfully wrestle with Mike and his message. Keep reading. This book just might take you out of your comfort zone, but that's right where many of us need to be led in order to be able to carefully and faithfully lead young people into the life-changing presence of God."

WALT MUELLER, PRESIDENT, CENTER FOR PARENT/YOUTH UNDERSTANDING AND AUTHOR OF *ENGAGING THE SOUL OF YOUTH CULTURE*

"Wow. Talk about stirring the pot! Mike King gets way out on some beautiful and truthful thin ice, naming many of the closely held wrong assumptions and faulty practices of modern youth ministry. Then he crosses to the other side of this thin ice, and suggests a path forward. Congrats to Mike, and to anyone willing to thoughtfully consider the ideas in this book!"

MARK OESTREICHER, PRESIDENT, YOUTH SPECIALTIES

To Al Metsker,

my first youth ministry mentor

who instilled in me a fiery passion

for young people to know Jesus . . .

and to Jessica,

who just finished her teenage years

and is still on the journey!

Contents

Reforma semper reformanda.

Introduction

Tylor was sixteen years old when he was tragically killed in an auto accident. Our youth ministry staff was devastated when we got the word, since he had been actively involved in leadership development. Little did we know the depth of his life and extent of his faith.

Tylor was a special young man, not because he was overflowing with talent, gifts and charm, but because he was a genuine disciple of Jesus Christ. He knew how to have fun even though he had adolescent issues to deal with like all teenagers. But Tylor comprehended the depth of faith that comes only by seeking the face of God. Out of his commitment to dwell in the presence of God, Tylor learned the importance of being a servant. It was through his service that so many were impacted by his life.

We weren't the only ones amazed by Tylor's life. So were his parents, Chris and Trish.

When Tylor left us, everyone from his life came together; it became a validation, a celebration, of the extraordinary life he lived, passionate for God. We knew he had an interest in and love for God. But perhaps like many parents, we didn't realize how deep his passion was. His death was an eye-opener.

At church, Tylor worked with the children's ministry. We thought it was just his way of avoiding the main service. Yet Tylor took to it naturally. It was like breathing to him.

From a young age, he'd always talked about being a professional athlete or an actor. But the January prior to his death, he informed us he was supposed to be a youth minister. Looking back now, it should have been clear to us. His life wasn't for show. His faith was real, and his heart was the heart of a youth pastor.

When he asked to serve on the teen staff at YouthFront Camp all summer long, once again we assumed less than the best—he's trying to get out of working. We asked him how he planned to find gas money to drive out to camp. He simply answered, "God's going to provide it." Somehow he knew God wanted him out there. We found out later how God had used him that summer. After his death, we heard from many teen staffers about how Tylor was always the listening ear, empathizing with others' thoughts and struggles.

Walking into Tylor's room after his death, we began to discover precious insights into his private life: his drawing, his journaling. We found he had been contemplating and questioning God. He had been looking for truth, reading through his Bible. It began to occur to us that neither of us had ever attempted his kind of search for the real God. Could it be that God was using Tylor's death to make us think more deeply about our own lives? About who God is?

Before Tylor's death we were searching for God—we thought. Learning of Tylor's deep spiritual life through his journal, his friends, and the Altar [a contemplative weekend of prayer and meditation on Scripture] made us realize that our own spirituality could be so much deeper. Our search for his faith has brought us closer to God.

Tylor was not the typical youth group kid who viewed church and a relationship with God as just another one of many things to fit into a busy life. Tylor was living a deep life with God nurtured by an environment I am referring to in this book as *presence-centered youth ministry.* Tylor was a young man with a full, authentic life in Jesus; his life still speaks very loudly to those who knew him.

According to data from denominations and research organizations, a majority of youth are walking away from the institutional church when they reach late adolescence, and most don't come back. But are they walking away from Jesus or from the way we do church and youth ministry? Young people haven't weighed Jesus in the balance and found his radical life and message irrelevant and uninspiring, but they are tired of church environments that allow the message of the gospel to be diminished. More and more young people are refusing to embrace the church cultures they have grown up in.

It's time for a thorough examination of our youth ministry philosophy and praxis. We need to create an authentic atmosphere for our young people to seek truth and discover who they are in Jesus. Youth ministry must move away from behavioral modification techniques and focus on creating environments for genuine spiritual transformation. We must guide young people into the presence of God.

The shift I propose begins with youth workers who live out of the wholeness of their own souls, who nurture a personal spirituality that makes Jesus Christ the center of everything. Youth need youth workers who dwell in the presence of God and are willing to walk along with them on the journey regardless of how often they are prone to personal detours.

I think the most important thing that could happen in youth ministry is to have passionate people working for it. I have seen so many youth workers in ministry who don't have a passion for it, and I think that hurts it more than anything else.

JESSICA, 17 YEARS OLD

In this book I will offer a critique of evangelical youth ministry practice and suggest correctives. This is done out of a passion for evangelicalism and love of the church. I believe much of this critique will also apply to a growing faction within postliberal mainline and evangelically oriented Catholic youth ministry. My hope is that this work will strengthen youth workers' convictions that young people need women and men of God in their lives—spiritual guides and mentors—first and foremost, over and above program specialists, social planners, cultural experts, comedians, behavioral therapists, event coordinators or video game specialists. As youth workers we must be passionate pursuers of God and invite youth to come with us on the journey.

I will examine Christian formation; discuss theological concerns and issues; look at the importance of nurturing environments that are safe for young people to discover their being and identity; explore the significance of creating sacred space for encountering God; examine ways to expose youth to spiritual practices without alarming them; all to help you be a spiritual guide to the youth God has brought into your life.

During the process of writing this book, I surveyed and talked with a hundred adolescents who have held on to a living faith at a time when so many of their peers are walking away from the church and faith. Throughout this book you will see the comments of these young people.

Hearing the passion and dreams of today's generation of young people for a dynamic church and a radical faith in Jesus fills me with optimism for the future. My prayer is that those of us working in the church and involved in youth ministry will nurture this passionate quest of young people instead of being an obstacle. Our calling as spiritual guides for adolescents is perhaps best expressed in this prayer by Thomas Merton:

> My Lord God I have no idea where I am going. I do not see the road ahead of me. I cannot know for certain where it will end. Nor do I really know myself, and the fact that I think I am following your will does not mean that I am actually doing so. But I believe that my desire to please you does in fact please you. And I hope that I have that desire in all that I am doing. I hope that I will never do anything apart from that desire. And I know that if I do this you will lead me by the right road though I may know nothing about it. Therefore will I trust you always though I may seem to be lost and in the shadow of death. I will not fear, for you are ever with me, and you will never leave me to face my perils alone.[1]

ACKNOWLEDGMENTS

I want to thank the YouthFront staff who passionately seek to live out the life and ministry I describe in this book—from the YouthFront Roundtable who love to celebrate with me on the mountain top but also walk with me through the valley of the shadow of death, to the YouthFront veterans who sacrifice to bring youth into a growing relationship with Jesus Christ, to the young staff, still in late adolescence, who graciously allow me to mentor and instruct them. All of you teach me how to be human and how to love life.

Thank you to all the adolescents involved in YouthFront who helped with this project: you inspire me.

I am so grateful for my friends and associates who engage with me in intense theological dialogue about what it means to live in the way of Jesus and what the Christian formation of adolescents should look like. Special thanks to Tony Jones, who has been a good friend and dialogue partner.

Thanks to my editor, Dave Zimmerman, for all your encouragement through this project. InterVarsity Press has been a blessing to work with.

A big thank-you to my church community at Jacob's Well. You have helped me love and believe in the church. Thanks to Tim Keel, my pastor, for your deep friendship and for fueling my passion for Jesus.

For all my friends: thanks for contributing in small and large ways to this project.

To Vicki, my wife of thirty years: I love you so much and can't imagine life without you.

I am so grateful for my children, Micah, Daniel and Jessica; daughters-in-law Anne and Lindsay; coming grandchildren, my parents, my siblings and my extended family. I am a blessed man!

Three Decades of Youth Ministry

I am past my thirtieth year of youth ministry. Sixty percent of my life has been devoted to it. I've just about seen it all. During the first seven years that I was a youth worker, sociologically speaking, I was an adolescent myself.

I used to be the handsome, young, gregarious, funny, athletic and very, very opinionated youth worker—and best of all, I had lots and lots of thick hair. A genuine kid magnet. I had the ears of thousands of students and together we were going to change the world. I just had to develop my skills for getting them saved.

I grew up in the Bible Belt, in a great family that occasionally attended church. We periodically went on family camping trips, and I remember lying under the stars often, deep in thought about where all of nature came from. When I hit adolescence and began thinking in more complex and abstract ways, I found myself overwhelmed many times with the concepts of God, the cosmos, eternity and the meaning of life, but I never wavered from an internal conviction that there has to be a God.

During this time my grandmother was diagnosed with cancer. In the middle of the night, agonizing in the hospital waiting room over the imminent loss of her own mother, my mom found among a stack of magazines a tract that presented four spiritual laws. She went to the hospital chapel, read the tract twice and had a conversion experience.

Mom announced to our family that we would begin to attend a Methodist church. One of the first events I remember was a lay witness mission. During this four-day event I was intrigued to hear people talk about God as their friend. We sat in a candlelit circle, and people shared about their personal experiences and relationships with God. I can still remember the physical, emotional and spiritual rush I got from these stories.

MY ADOLESCENCE

Evaluating my life between the ages of fifteen and eighteen makes me very thankful that I attended the mainline church I did. This church was full of people who accepted me just as I was. I had a lot of energy. I'm an adventurer, and I needed space to explore, to check things out and to figure out who I was.

I made a lot of mistakes. Sometimes I drank too much. I remember going to church several times after a night of partying. My head would be throbbing, but I remember praying, "God, I'm sorry. I know you're disappointed with me. Help me to not do that again." Of course, the adults in my church didn't approve of my behavior. However, I remember never once being looked down upon, scorned or judged. I just remember being loved, encouraged, valued and accepted.

In the Sunday services I was especially drawn to the liturgy. Praying the Lord's Prayer, reciting the Apostles' Creed, singing the *Glory Be* and the *Doxology* were so meaningful to me. Even though I was caught up in figuring out my identity and making stupid mistakes in the process, I knew that God was working in my life. I look back at the environment of this church and thank God I was in a place that allowed me to discover who I was and who God was.

During my junior and senior year in high school, I passionately engaged in a lot of typical adolescent experimentation that no doubt had my parents quite concerned. They worked on me until I finally agreed to attend a youth rally. I was impressed to see more than one thousand teenagers there. These Saturday night rallies were filled with enthusiastic teenagers, seemingly excited about their faith in Jesus. I made friends and became a regular attendee, even becoming part of a drama team. Staff members began to give me attention.

I remember like yesterday when I was first confronted by their conservative mindset, something I had never encountered before. It was April, and I made some comment about senior prom. A couple of the kids looked at me like I had just suggested we worship Satan. When they left, one of the girls on the music team said, "I'd like to go to my senior prom, but we have to agree not to go to school dances if we're serving on a ministry team."[1] I remember being conflicted over this issue. I did make it to prom, but I didn't want to be ostracized, so I shared with several of my new Christian friends that "I only did one dance."

MY CHANGING VIEWS

As I became more involved in this ministry, the big issue was everyone's insistence that I needed to get out of the church I had attended for years and get into a "Bible-preaching, Bible-believing church." Reluctantly I finally left, but soon I was starting to feel righteous about my decision; after all, *many are called but few are chosen*. I wanted to be a spiritual giant. I soon began working full time with this youth ministry and enrolled in their Bible institute.

I was told that the important thing about being a biblical Christian was living by the fundamentals of the faith. I earned a master's degree from Liberty University and often preached there. I became a proud fundamentalist, willing to do battle against liberals and emphasizing the "historic fundamentals" (the virgin birth, Christ's substitutionary atonement, the inerrancy of Scripture, Christ's bodily resurrection and the second coming of Jesus). I was taught—and in turn taught young people—that certainty about all truth would enable them to live a victorious Christian life.

The emphasis was on using our minds to know the Bible. (Actually we only took certain parts of the Bible seriously; we reserved many of Jesus' words for some future perfect world, when we would have some new supernatural ability to live out what he was saying.) Our emotions and experiences were not to be trusted; they would surely lead us astray. There was little latitude for other interpretations of Scripture and no room for emotional experiences. God just didn't work that way.

The cognitive understanding of what was important in Scripture seemed to be structured around our cultural tool kit. I was asked to cut my worldly long hair and shave off my mustache so I would be a good testimony to young people, because Jesus would not have a mustache and long hair if he lived in our culture. We measured our spirituality by avoiding sins on a top-one-hundred sin list: alcohol, smoking, secularism, cussing, appearances of evil, and of course, the Democratic Party. I went twelve years without stepping into a movie theater. The devil was in everything: your pants, the music, the public schools, anything secular. In fact, *secular* and *demonic* were interchangeable words.

I loved my fellow staff members, and they loved me. We were passionate for God. As youth workers, we believed that if we avoided all the things of the world, teenagers would line up to have what we had. I spent a lot of time projecting an image of having everything together, and I expected the kids who looked up to me to emulate my lifestyle.

NUMBERS, CULTURE AND DECISIONS

In the early days I engaged in activity for God aggressively. I defined my success by the number of teenagers who made salvation decisions. We kept a running list of teenagers who prayed the sinner's prayer—even if they had gotten saved before. I articulated lists of do's and don'ts as a catechism of ultimate spirituality. I gave messages against rock music to shock and convince teenagers that they ought to feel guilty about interaction with this popular culture medium. I wouldn't let my sons watch *He-Man* or *Teenage Mutant Ninja Turtles* because they used special powers, which was evil.

I memorized great portions of Scripture because "the Word of God does the work of God." I learned how to prooftext with the best of them: if a teenager ever questioned me on what it means to live a holy life, I could bury them under a barrage of quoted verses. After all, how can you argue with the Word of God? I had it all down. I was a "professional" youth worker.

To hone my skills on getting teenagers into heaven, I went through a one-week training course called "How to Give an Invitation." We studied how to remove "sales resistance" for the Holy Spirit. Oh, we knew the Holy Spirit could do what he wanted, but why make it harder than necessary for a teenager to come forward?

We were taught psychological methodology to get teenagers to make a decision. We knew when to have them bow their heads and close their eyes. We knew what kind of music to use and when to cue it. We weren't to say, "Is there anyone here who wants to get saved?"

because that makes everyone think they might be the only one and they would be too embarrassed to respond. Instead, we were instructed to ask, "How many of you want to get saved?" Furthermore, we were not to respond until several hands went up so we could say, "Yes, I see that hand, and that hand. Yes, another, and another. Yes, I see that hand and that one. There's another." When you get on a roll, the numbers go up.

The next steps were to pray for them and then carefully instruct them how they were to all to come forward at the same time to the prayer room so they could get saved. "You can know for sure, in just a few minutes that you will go to heaven when you die." If I'd been given a dollar for every time I asked, "If you died tonight, would you go to heaven?" during my first fifteen years in youth ministry, I would have an impressive portfolio.

IN THE CATHEDRAL

One of my fellow youth worker friends left to attend Moody Bible Institute, which was considered liberal for our culture. I went to visit him in Chicago, at the time the largest city I had ever been to. We were walking downtown when we passed a huge Catholic cathedral. I had never seen anything like this before, so I said to my friend, "Let's go in."

The magnificence of the cathedral overwhelmed me. I took it all in: the stained glass windows, the statues, the marble, the art, the incense, people spread throughout the cathedral praying. It brought back memories of my Methodist church. It was awesome, even transcendent. All of it drew me into the presence of God. I sat down and started to pray.

My encounter with the divine was soon shattered by the sound of my friend's voice. He was standing at the altar, projecting loud enough to gain the attention of everyone in the cathedral: "For there is one God; there is also one mediator between God and humankind, Christ Jesus, himself human" (1 Tim 2:5). When he finished he walked down the center of the aisle and motioned for me to come, as if we needed to escape before they burned us at the stake.

When we returned to the safety of the sidewalk, I was speechless. Proudly my friend stated, "We have to remind them that there is only one mediator, and it's not the Pope." He reminded me that our experiences can deceive us; after all, "God's presence is not in a church like that."

These attitudes and events are painful to share, but I'm doing it because much of North American evangelicalism is still using these same tactics today. The tactics have a twenty-first-century sophistication to them, but they're driven by the same theological thinking (you'll find more about this in the next two chapters). Even though I was faithfully trying to follow Jesus and passionate about reaching teenagers with the good news, many of my efforts were actually detrimental to the Christian formation of adolescents.

ANOTHER TURN

During the early 1990s it painfully, slowly dawned on me that for the previous dozen years or so I had lived a very pharisaical spirituality. This awareness led to repentance and the beginning of a radical restructuring of everything I thought about Christianity. Today, I'm in remission, a recovering Pharisee.

I began calling myself an *evangelical,* which had previously been a negative label to me. A search for new, like-minded friends and youth workers led me to attend my first Youth Specialties National Youth Worker Convention in 1993. Youth Specialties had always been on the bad-guys list, but from the moment I walked into this environ-

I think a lot of youth are fed up with Christians and frustrated with their church experience as a result. The majority of people don't have a problem with Jesus or the Bible but with the people who call themselves Christians and who don't mirror Christ's actions.

KRISTEN, 18 YEARS OLD

ment of passion, not only for youth ministry but for life, I felt affirmed, renewed and eager to become a better youth worker and a more passionate follower of Jesus.[2]

Shortly into the year 2000 my journey with Christ took another significant turn. In 1999 the Holy Spirit began to open my life with God into a deeper walk and a renewed passion. I believe my "first love" for Jesus was rekindled. At the same time I was becoming increasingly frustrated with my church experience and environment which seemed to be pretty consistent with many other churches that I worked with or were familiar with. I was tired of seeing young people damaged by a brand of Christianity that was increasingly arrogant and mean-spirited. We in the church have spent a lot of effort to define worldliness as smoking, drinking, popular culture and so on, but if we took the message of Jesus seriously, shouldn't we have included sins like greed, debt, materialism and gluttony? I had been promoting a Christianity that accepts overworking, overeating and apathy toward social justice. I had been a part of retrofitting Christianity for the American dream.

I became connected with others who had similar spiritual backgrounds. Being drawn to so many who were on the same quest seemed, at the time, to be quite mystical, but looking back it has become apparent that there were just so many people asking the same questions and dealing with the same issues. I believe the Holy Spirit was stirring hearts and minds.

Why are so many people walking away from the church? Why is North American evangelicalism so aligned with a political agenda?

What presuppositions do we bring to our theological pursuits? What does a missional church look like at the dawn of the twenty-first century? What kinds of ecclesiological and theological corrections need to happen? I let go of much I once thought was essential and embraced a journey to pursue God. I wanted to walk intimately with Jesus.

I'm not saying I've finally arrived. In fact, I probably have more questions now than ever before. At the same time, I have never been so fulfilled and enthusiastic about ministry and passionate about my life pilgrimage with Christ. I've gone through a series of profoundly influential experiences, questions, relationships, theological paradigm shifts, pilgrimages, academic pursuits and encounters with God. Viewing life as a journey and seeing faith as steadfastness over a long period, along with a renewed passionate pursuit of Jesus, has awakened me to the joy of life with God. More than anything I want to rediscover my first love, to rethink what it means to be a follower of Jesus Christ. I want to live a life of intimacy with God—to be aware of and dwell in the presence of God in a consistent and transformational way.[3]

Dysfunctional Evangelical Youth Ministry

ecently I met in Washington, D.C., with the leaders of more than forty national youth organizations. During our two days together, I kept hearing comments like these:

- We are losing the culture war against our teenagers.
- We have to take back this country for God.
- America has become the most debauched nation.

Several attendees were worked up over the statistic that more than 80 percent of people who grow up in the church leave it when they hit their twenties.[1] At the same time that we're seeing flight from the church, however, interest in spirituality is at an all-time high among young people. Consider the data released by the Higher Education Research Institute at UCLA. In polling 112,232 freshmen from 236 colleges and universities, they discovered that eight out of ten attend religious services. More than 80 percent say they are very interested in spirituality. More than two-thirds of them pray. In fact, the UCLA study suggests that this generation may be one of the most caring and unselfish generations of the last century.

We're all concerned about the number of young people who are walking away from church. According to Barna Research, 58 percent of today's teenagers who attend church regularly won't be there by their thirtieth birthday. Many leaders in youth ministry seem convinced that the solution to this exodus from the church is to do what we've done in the past—rail on sin, hire the loudest evangelists, pump in more fun, condemn the evil media—only with more intensity. Others suggest trying alternative ideas, perhaps even radical reformation of youth ministry philosophy and praxis: If the way we're doing youth ministry is failing, let's creatively rethink how youth ministry is done.

These aren't evil, secular youth who have examined Jesus Christ and found him insufficient. We have young people who are responding more and more to the call to embrace a radical faith of service to Christ. This generation is looking for adult leadership that will believe in them, listen to them, understand them and model being authentic followers of Jesus Christ. More youth workers are beginning to understand that only when we eliminate the ineffective practices of the past twenty-five years will more of our youth be willing to dive into the dangerous wonder of living in the advancing kingdom of God. The notion of youth workers as entertainers and program directors must give way to youth workers as authentic shepherds, spiritual guides with a holy anointing to lead youth into the presence of God.

> Some young people stop going to church because the church they are attending is stuck in the way that they do things and not open to suggestions or ideas. There is no life there. I believe youth are devalued in many of today's churches.
>
> **CHAD, COLLEGE STUDENT**

DECONSTRUCTING EVANGELICALISM

Before we start to construct what a healthier or corrective youth ministry might look like, let's examine the present state of evangelicalism.

So many of my friends are frustrated with their church experience. Many of them have left churches because of the way they were treated in their youth group, not only by peers but also by adults.

STEPHANIE, 19 YEARS OLD

This is not just about youth ministry; it is in a broader sense about ecclesiological issues.

Robert Webber joked in an interview about the history of Christianity in "four easy steps": "The Christian church began as a mission in Jerusalem. It moved to Rome and became an institution. It moved to Europe and became a culture. It moved across the ocean and became a big business."[2]

Presence-centered youth ministry is about deconstructing the big business of North American evangelicalism and returning to the missional nature of ministry in the way of Jesus. We need to examine and critique present-day North American evangelicalism out of love for the church and a desire for it to be truly evangelical.

Evangelicalism, in the broadest and earliest sense of the term, is connected to the Reformation of the sixteenth century and is simply another way of describing Protestantism. The core aspect of evangelicalism, in this sense, is the Reformation tenet of *sola fide,* which focuses on a personal relationship with Jesus Christ as Lord and Savior who offers salvation by grace through *faith alone.*

The meaning of *evangelicalism* narrowed somewhat when it became a more specific description of the great awakenings of the eighteenth and nineteenth centuries. New and significant emphasis was placed on personal conversion, piety and zealous evangelism. Many hail John Wesley as the first modern-day evangelical.

The term *evangelical* morphed into a new definition in North America during the early twentieth century. Fundamentalism had emerged as a hardcore reaction against the influence of liberalism and German higher criticism (rooted in the work of theologians such as

Friedrich Schleiermacher, Ludwig Andreas Feuerbach and Rudolf Bultmann) raised questions about the historical reliability of the Scriptures. Those who were not comfortable being aligned with the fundamentalist reaction called themselves new evangelicals and later simply evangelicals. Increasingly this movement developed DNA around the passion of evangelism and the proliferation of parachurch organizations. D. G. Hart, in his book *Deconstructing Evangelicalism: Conservative Protestantism in the Age of Billy Graham,* describes Billy Graham as the first evangelical pope and inerrancy of Scripture as its defining doctrinal belief.

North American evangelicalism increasingly took on a specific political agenda; today many people consider evangelicals to be closely aligned with the political right.

BETTER THAN PROSTITUTES, BARELY

The contemporary view of evangelicals is grim. Tony Campolo describes a word association survey: the word *Jesus* evoked responses such as *Savior, God, forgiving* and *love.* Meanwhile, responses to the word *evangelical* leaned toward descriptions like *mean-spirited, harsh, scornful* and *arrogant.*[3] The Barna Research Group released a nationwide survey in December 2002 that further documents the sad image of evangelicals that non-Christian adults hold. Asked to rate eleven groups of people, non-Christian adults placed evangelicals in tenth place. The only group that rated worse were prostitutes.[4]

Michael Spencer wrote a well-written and insightful evaluation of the hostility that seems to be

I believe that unloving, legalistic, "traditional," church-going Christians have pushed away a lot of people in my generation. I think we realize that a hardcore faith that really costs us something is what will capture our imagination. I don't think many churches are ready for that kind of expression of faith.

EMILY, COLLEGE STUDENT

commonly felt toward evangelicals, called "Why Do They Hate Us?" Here are some of his main points:

- We endorse a high standard of conduct for others and then largely excuse ourselves from a serious pursuit of such a life.

- Our piety is mostly public. We love others to see what God is doing in our lives.

- Many of us relate to others with an obvious—or thinly disguised—agenda. In other words, those who work with us or go to school with us think we are "up to something."

- Many of us are bizarrely shallow and legalistic about minute matters. We are not as healthy and happy as we portray ourselves.

- We may deny that we have made God into a political, financial or cultural commodity, but the world knows better.

- We are too slow to separate ourselves from what's wrong. It's clear to many that we no longer have the cutting-edge moral sense of Martin Luther King Jr. or William Wilberforce.

- We take ourselves far too seriously and appear to be opposed to normal life. What normal, healthy people find laughable, we find threatening and often label with the ridiculous label "of the devil."[5]

> The majority of people I know who have left the church left because they were burned by a former church or other Christians. This is usually due to legalism in the church or people who claim the name of Jesus but live in sin, bitterness, contempt, et cetera.
>
> **MOE, COLLEGE STUDENT**

It seems clear that North American evangelicals are held in contempt by a growing segment of the population. The moralizing message that is communicated by prominent evangelical voices is being viewed as duplicitous and hypocritical. Fortunately, I don't think that Jesus is getting the blame for this reputation. Peter Glover explains,

> When we observe just what is often served up as "evangelical" fare today, it is hardly surprising that the world has the impression it does. For them "evangelical" means the TV evangelist with his wealth-seeking "name it and claim it gospel." It means gullible evangelicals falling over themselves to hear fake healers and false prophets for their own emotional gratification. It means carefree "happy clappers" oblivious to the concerns of ordinary life, and evangelical antiquarians who separate themselves entirely from the real world. Of course, this is not true historic evangelicalism at all, but a pale modern imitation. But it is chiefly what the world sees, and has become a hindrance to the true gospel.[6]

More and more church leaders, theologians and historians are concerned that the North American evangelical church is pursuing an agenda that harkens back to the era of Christendom which emerged in the centuries following Constantine's Edict of Milan in A.D. 313. This edict made Christianity legal and eventually the official religion of the Roman Empire. As a result, the lines of distinction between church and state were blurred. D. G. Hart argues that evangelicalism in North America has morphed into something that is damaging to historic Christianity. "As much as the American public thinks of evangelicalism as the 'old-time religion,' whether positively or negatively, this expression of Christianity has severed most ties to the ways and beliefs of Christians living in previous eras. For that reason, it needs to be deconstructed."[7]

The tension between being *of* the world but not *in* the world has always been a challenging dynamic for true pilgrim followers of

Jesus, but it is possible to radically live out the faith of Jesus and have the goodwill of people as we know first-century Christians did:

Day by day, as they spent much time together in the temple, they broke bread at home and ate their food with glad and generous hearts, praising God and *having the goodwill of all the people*. And day by day the Lord added to their number those who were being saved. (Acts 2:46-47, emphasis mine)

It is important to engage in careful theological reflection to know whom we are really representing and not abuse the name of Jesus in order to advance our own agendas, whether they are religious, political or social.[8] The church of Jesus Christ has survived two thousand years of threats, transitions, paradigm shifts, political trends, social upheavals, scientific discoveries and attacks. The church has not only survived during change and transition, it's thrived. We honor all reformers of the church of Jesus Christ when we continue the process of theological reflection, critique of praxis, pursuit of missional passion and obedience to the Holy Spirit at work in the world. *Reformed, always reforming* should be our mindset.

PROBLEMS WITHIN EVANGELICAL YOUTH MINISTRY

Several of the problems D. G. Hart examines in *Deconstructing Evangelicalism* have specific ramifications for youth ministry.

Succession. North American evangelicalism has been negatively impacted by underdeveloped theology and praxis for passing the faith from one generation to the next.

Christianity of the evangelical variety has historically struggled with the question of succession. How does the conversion experience become a model for nurture? Countless evangelical converts, having left behind a life of sin and irreligion, face a difficult task when thinking about passing on the faith to their offspring. Do they encourage their children to pursue the life they did, one of rebellion followed by the ecstasy of regeneration, so that their sons and daughters will come to genuine faith? Not likely. Much more common is the decision to rear their children in the beliefs and practices of the faith, even when such instruction and nurture flatly contradict the model of the conversion experience. After all, turning to God's mercy is much easier after a life of drugs and sex than it is after a wholesome upbringing of church attendance, family devotions, and Bible memorization.[9]

My conversion experience was radical and involved a major course correction in my life. My kids, however, grew up in the church. We tried to develop creative ways to mark the progress of their developing faith. We created ways for them to symbolically move into new facets of their faith journeys.

Years ago I was invited by a Jewish family to attend their son's bar mitzvah in the ruins of the oldest synagogue in the world on top of Masada. My friend and I were the only Gentiles in attendance. I was so moved by the deep significance of this rite of passage that I went back and made a ten-year plan with my wife to have our children's baptism service in the land of the Bible to mark the succession of their faith. Once they all hit their teen years, we held a special baptism service in the Jordan River. Commissioned by our church, I baptized our three kids in a moving ceremony surrounded by twenty-five of their friends.

Of course, we don't have to go to Israel to mark the succession of faith and to emphasize this rite of passage, but we do need to do more than a yearly youth service (if that) or a graduation Sunday. Few evangelical churches have seen the need for or developed a catechism to systematically approach succession with their youth. We need to seriously give attention to this matter.

Lack of tradition. Another concern within evangelicalism is an unhealthy view of the importance of tradition. We will visit the topic of tradition extensively in a later chapter, but I will state here that it's a significant problem. Hart acknowledges that evangelicalism is largely hostile to tradition.

> Unlike older forms of Christianity that pass on the faith to new generations through the family and churchly means of birth, baptism, catechism, and worship, evangelicalism locates the primary mechanic of religious identity in the sovereign individual, a move that is about as modern and anti-traditional as can be.[10]

Looking into Christian history and thought has not been of much interest to older evangelicals, but it is something that young people seem to be fascinated with. The younger generation has the mindset to view the history of Christianity as a part of their family story. Tradition, creeds and practices are much more easily respected as family heirlooms by current adolescent Christians. Youth are rediscovering prayer practices, lectio divina, historic creeds, liturgy and prayer postures, along with other meaningful rituals that have been abandoned for centuries.

Unfortunately, many times the older generation responds to these heirlooms with fear. I recently met with a group of parents who were concerned that their kids were meditating, practicing lectio divina and reciting the Apostles' Creed. One of the overly zealous mothers claimed that most of these practices were Neo-Pagan in origin. Her rhetoric was softened after a historical explanation of these practices, but she still pled for us to use a word other than *meditation* to describe what they were doing. I offered several verses that encourage meditation on Scripture (for example, Ps 1:2; 19:14; Josh 1:8) and explained, "This is our word, and it's used more than sixty times in Scripture. If we have to redeem it, we will, but it's our word."

At YouthFront camps we observe midday prayer, a contemplative and liturgical time of prayer involving the whole community. This fixed-time prayer is unfamiliar to many evangelicals but is deeply connected to Christianity and is, in fact, fully established in the Hebrew world of the Old Testament. (A fuller explanation of fixed-hour prayer is found in chapter eight.)

Age segregation. Another huge problem within evangelical ecclesiological practice is the propensity to segregate youth ministry from the rest of the church. Even though many churches pledge during infant dedications or baptisms to help raise a child as a community of believers, too often the next time the child is before the congregation is to honor them for graduating from high school. This is frighteningly dysfunctional and removes one of the most effective practices of spiritual formation, interaction between generations. Unfortunately, much of youth ministry practice places value on creating youth centers and programs, resulting—by default or intent—in separated generations.

> I love the theology in the prayers we recite during midday prayer and how I am in the midst of the body of Christ declaring prayers that have been spoken throughout history.
>
> **LAURA, COLLEGE STUDENT**

How do we expect to fulfill the biblical model of younger women and men learning from older women and men?

Urge the younger men to be self-controlled. Show yourself in all respects a model of good works, and in your teaching show integrity, gravity, and sound speech that cannot be censured. (Tit 2:6-8)

Too often the only adult the youth in a church have interaction with is a youth worker. The prototype for this youth worker is frequently a recent college graduate who is nearly an adolescent himself. Tom Sine describes the scenario this way: "How do we typically conduct youth ministry in our middle-class congregations? Hire a guy with a sports car to run activity-driven programs to entertain the young people and keep them busy, distracted, and out of trouble."[11]

My wife and I are involved at Jacob's Well, a six-year-old church in Kansas City. We have around a thousand who attend on Sundays, approximately half of these in their twenties. Even though we have quite a few teenagers, we don't have an official youth group. I like to say we have a youth ministry but no youth group. When we began to attend Jacob's Well, our only child living with us was Jessica (sixteen years old at the time). It was wonderful to have her with us, actually sitting together in church. She had a mentor, Jaime, who was twenty-five years old. Jaime spent time with her and helped her through many challenging high school issues.

> I have been blessed to have several adults who came alongside me during middle and high school and take me seriously. Kids need adults who want to be involved in their spiritual development.
>
> **KRISTEN, 18 YEARS OLD**

Looking back, this has been the best experience we have had involving church and youth ministry, including the years when I was the youth pastor for my own boys.

Don't get me wrong, I'm not necessarily advocating we eliminate youth pastors and youth ministry. I'm saying we must give these issues serious consideration and begin to reimagine more holistic, healthy ways to offer youth ministry in our churches. Our teenagers need to be around, to interact and live life with people in their faith community who represent all the generations. Wise is the youth worker who makes this an important value for youth ministry.

Decisionism. I mark my involvement in conservative evangelicalism with the major emphasis on making the decision. This emphasis continued to be the main concern for most of my youth ministry. This decision was described in various ways: accepting Jesus Christ as Savior, making a decision for Christ, getting saved or deciding to give your life to Jesus.

The decision was accomplished by getting the teenager to pray the sinner's prayer. "Lord Jesus, come into my heart. I know that I am a sinner. Please forgive me for all my sins. Thank you for dying for me on the cross. Take me home to heaven when I die. In Jesus' name, Amen!" Of course, we stressed that they had to mean it with all their heart. This was always followed with a proclamation similar to this: "If you prayed that prayer and really meant it, you will go to heaven when you die." The second most important decision was *the dedication.* Dedication decisions involved giving one's all to Jesus, as if the first decision wasn't able to accomplish that. The third decision was *the rededication,* which could be made over and over again.

I wish I could say that the emphasis on decisionism as a primary spiritual formation tool is no longer prevalent within evangelical youth ministry, but I'm afraid that wouldn't be an accurate statement. I was sharing my concern about decisionism with a pastor from a

> Most adults in the church underestimate students, both intellectually and spiritually. Too many adults don't expect teenagers to act or think in mature ways, so they think it's OK to wait for serious spiritual formation to happen. But so many young people are ready to jump into a radical faith and want to be mentored by adults who take them seriously.
>
> **MOE, COLLEGE STUDENT**

large church. His question was, How else could someone become a Christian?

My answer is that people can respond in obedience to the call that Jesus always makes: "Come, follow me." I know this seems like a decision, but the decisions we make being a follower of Jesus are so different than the formulaic nature of the sinner's prayer. We cheapen what it means to be a disciple, a follower of Jesus, when we give kids the idea that praying a sinner's prayer settles things once and for all. We make thousands of decisions as we follow Christ.

We must remember that when Jesus invited his disciples to follow him, they didn't immediately figure out what that meant. By the time the following incident took place in Caesarea Philippi, the disciples had been following Jesus for approximately eighteen months:

> Now when Jesus came into the district of Caesarea Philippi, he asked his disciples, "Who do people say that the Son of Man is?" And they said, "Some say John the Baptist, but others Elijah, and still others Jeremiah or one of the prophets." He said to them, "But who do you say that I am?" Simon Peter answered, "You are the Messiah, the Son of the living God." And Jesus answered him, "Blessed are you, Simon son of Jonah! For flesh and blood has not revealed this to you, but my Father in heaven." (Mt 16:13-17)

Jesus would not have been considered a good youth pastor in most of our evangelical churches. Jesus was obviously willing to give followers the time and space to understand. Too often the expectation is that the youth who come to our churches better know by the end of their first experience with us that Jesus Christ is the Son of the living God. The rush to get kids to make a decision for Jesus takes away the important process of counting the cost of being his follower. When was the last time you encouraged a young person to not make a decision, to count the cost before making such an important, life-altering choice?

Jesus tells his disciples, "Unless you eat the flesh of the Son of Man and drink his blood, you have no life in you" (Jn 6:53). Many complained that this teaching was too difficult, and some turned away from following him. But Simon Peter spoke for the twelve: "Lord, to whom can we go? You have the words of eternal life. We have *come to believe* and know that you are the Holy One of God" (Jn 6:68-69, emphasis mine). We must move away from premature and manipulated decision-making and instead create environments that allow for time and space, where youth are repeatedly ushered into the presence of God. We must allow transformation to come by the Holy Spirit instead of by gimmickry, tricks and manipulation.

In my first two decades of youth ministry, it was unthinkable to not have an invitation at youth ministry gatherings. Now I haven't given a formal "hand raising" invitation in years. I'm focused on allowing young people to see what being a follower of Jesus is all about and trusting the Holy Spirit to transform them when the time is right. Allowing youth to belong in our communities without pressuring them results in authentic decisions to follow Jesus.

> My youth pastor was awesome and allowed me to experience God and develop spiritually as God led me, not at the pace he thought I should grow.
>
> **ELIZABETH, COLLEGE STUDENT**

WHAT HAS HAPPENED TO CHRISTIAN FORMATION?

The problems discussed in this chapter are directly related to the lack of a consistent focus on—and valuing of—classic Christian formation. The Christian formation of youth will be severely retarded without the holistic involvement of the entire congregation. The problems we have with the succession of the faith to younger generations are directly impacted by the lack of Christian formation involving the whole congregation. An emphasis on decisionism has in many ways been a cheap substitute for the serious and vital importance of Christian formation. Pressing or manipulating teenagers to make the decision to accept Christ can be accomplished rather easily, but a commitment to Christian formation for a lifetime is another matter.

In my seminary studies of Christian history and thought I discovered and rediscovered many wonderful heirlooms of our faith. Over two thousand years of church history, believers have developed practices, disciplines and ways to be conformed into the likeness of Christ. I have found adolescents respond enthusiastically when I introduce ancient practices, sometimes with a contemporary twist. Many of these Christian formation practices (covered in later chapters), however, have been forgotten or dismissed out of an evangelical scorn of tradition. A dominant expression of North American evangelicalism in the last decade and a half has been the seeker-sensitive movement, which operates under the assumption that if Christians are going to relate to contemporary people we must make them feel comfortable when they come to church. This has led to new terminology that seekers will understand, the shedding of tradition and traditional practices, the removal of religious symbols from our places of worship so that they resemble a community center instead of a church, and the creation of music and messages that feel more like popular culture.

On the other hand, outside the church building many of us try to distinguish ourselves from mainstream culture so people will know we are different. (Maybe odd or weird would be more accurate descriptions.) Michael Spencer suggests that in so doing we come off as opposed to normal life. Is it such a big deal that Christians are offended at so many things others consider funny? I'll admit, it is a small thing, but it is one of the reasons ordinary people don't like us.[12]

In reality, at first glance we should be largely indistinguishable in culture. We should have representatives in every cultural category, not because we have strategically targeted the sports crowd, the country and western music crowd, or the intelligentsia with our missionaries, but because followers of Jesus may well have those interests and fit into those crowds.

People shouldn't be able to take one look at us and say, "They have to be Christians." They should see Jesus in us through the encounters we have with them, which means they should have to get to know us before they recognize our uniqueness in Christ. Our lives as the church scattered—our lives outside of church buildings—should shatter many improper but deserved stereotypes of what Christians are.

> Are churches in North America doing a good job of imitating the life and message of Jesus? No. We get concerned with luxuries and attracting people by the looks of our buildings. We've forgotten the power of God.
>
> **AMY, COLLEGE STUDENT**

According to Miroslav Volf, it should not be until they encounter the church gathered—until they come to our churches—that non-Christians sense something is different about followers of Jesus. In *After Our Likeness: The Church as the Image of Trinity,* Volf discusses the importance of our places of worship as places of transcendence, places that seem different and peculiar to those outside of the church.[13] It should be a bit odd and peculiar for visitors to enter our sanctuaries and engage in worship. This isn't bad. It's good. It shows that we are a subculture that's distinct. The cross, the crucifix, the baptismal pool or font, Communion, liturgies, common prayer—all these symbols identify us as a community of the people of God.

Young people love logos and symbols, so why have we shielded them from the symbols of our faith? They are fascinated by the stories of family history, traditions and spiritual practices. More than anything, they need to enter into the presence of God. They are transformed through it. If we are going to see this happen, many things

	Traditional Evangelicals (1950-1975)	Pragmatic Evangelicals (1975-2000)	Younger Evangelicals (2000-)
Theological Commitment	Rational worldview	Therapy Answers needs	Christianity as a community of faith Ancient/Reformaton
Apologetics Style	Evidential Foundational	Christianity as meaning-giver Experiential Personal faith	Embrace the metanarrative Embodied apologetic Communal faith
Ecclesial Paradigm	Constantinian church Civil religion	Culturally sensitive church	Missional church Countercultural
Church Style	Neighborhood churches Rural	Megachurch Suburban Market-targeted	Small church Back to cities Intercultural
Leadership Style	Pastor-centered	Managerial model CEO	Team ministry Priesthood of all
Youth Ministry	Church-centered programs	Outreach programs Weekend fun retreats	Prayer, Bible study, worship, social action
Education	Sunday school Information centered	Target generational groups and needs	Intergenerational formation in community
Spirituality	Keep the rules	Prosperity and success	Embodiment
Worship	Traditional	Contemporary	Convergence
Art	Restrained	Art as illustration	Incarnational
Evangelism	Mass evangelism	Seeker service	Process evangelism
Activism	Beginnings of evangelical social action	Need-driven social action (divorce groups, drug rehab)	Rebuild cities and neighborhoods

Evangelical shifts. Taken from Robert Webber, *The Younger Evangelicals* (Grand Rapids: Baker, 2002).

will have to change concerning how we do youth ministry, how we do Christian formation, indeed how we do church.

Robert Webber, in his book *The Younger Evangelicals,* summarizes the state of evangelicalism in the last one hundred years and focuses on the significant shift among young people that is under way. Webber uses the term *younger evangelicals* to describe this generation of young people who want to reexamine what being a follower of Jesus and what being a church is all about. A helpful chart from Webber's book (see p. 40) shows shifts in expressions of spirituality, theological practice and mindset, missional focus, and worship changes over three generations of evangelicals.

THREE

A Convergence of Fronts

Somewhere out over the Atlantic Ocean in a 747, I was trying to doze in the midst of gentle turbulence, like a baby being bounced in its mother's arms. Suddenly the plane shook violently and dropped nearly a thousand feet. Fully awake now and seeing the look on the flight attendant's face, I assumed this wasn't normal. After the plane stabilized, the captain explained that we had been impacted by a convergence of fronts—weather, jet stream and turbulence from another 747 flying a few miles ahead of us. He explained he would slow down and put some distance between us and the plane in front of us and assured us that we were OK.

I usually love the convergence of fronts. The beach where land and water meet. The rapids created by two rivers coming together. An electrical storm caused by warm air and cool air colliding. I remember watching rain clouds moving toward me and some friends. We were fascinated by the approach of the ominous-looking clouds, and though we knew we should seek shelter, no one wanted to leave. As the clouds came closer, we could feel the atmosphere change and see the rain falling in what seemed like a solid wall. We decided to wait until the last possible moment to outrun the rain to shelter. Closer and closer it came until someone finally yelled *run*. We took off laughing, our adrenaline pumping, with the rain gaining on us as we took each step. We made it to shelter just as we felt the first raindrops. A few seconds more and we would have been drenched. What an exhilarating experience!

CONVERGING FRONTS: Epistemological, Ecclesiological, Theological, Philosophical, Scientific and Sociological Shifts

In some ways I feel like I am experiencing all these same emotions—fear, excitement, uncertainty, wonder and awe—when I consider the converging fronts we're experiencing in the world we live in today.

- We are experiencing the final stages of the domination of modern rationalism birthed in the Enlightenment. This reality is crashing into the dynamics of what this postmodern age means for science, theology, Scripture and truth.

- We're experiencing ecclesiological shifts related to missional and theological issues impacted by postmodernity and the ongoing effect of postreformation reaction and overreactions.

- Newtonian physics that once seemed certain to yield the answers to life's greatest questions—What is the purpose of life? What is the future of the cosmos?—has been challenged and reframed by discoveries in quantum physics. Twenty years ago, Nobel-prizewinners were declaring that we were about to get all the remaining mysteries of the cosmos figured out. Now they're telling us that quantum mechanics has opened new realms of mystery, pointing to the reality of a supreme being or force—a Creator. New theological questions are surfacing within the context of quantum physics that are all together amazing, frightening, awesome and exciting. If you think your kids aren't

interested in theology, try engaging them with this emerging
scientific-theological dialogue.

- We're seeing generational shifts and changes related specifically
  to youth ministry. Many youth workers were trained to minister
  to Gen-Xers and now find themselves with a Millennial generation that is radically different. No doubt these convergences of
  generational fronts are creating a significant amount of turbulence.

I won't be systematically addressing the issue of postmodernity;
others have already tackled that task. But I will say that I view postmodernity as an opportunity to evaluate theological, ecclesiological
and epistemological overreactions to rationalism. The effort to establish certainty in everything connected to Christianity has domesti-
cated our faith. I want to know God, not just by Scripture, reason and
thought, but also by heart and soul and through experiences and
within my community.

Converging fronts that involve change always create turbulence.
And yet, change has been a part of life since the beginning of time.
As cycles and transitions unfold, we are responsible to do the on-
going work of theology and contextualization of the good news.

We only need to examine other comparable times in history to see
how foolish we can be. Copernicus and Galileo were vigorously at-
tacked for suggesting that the earth was not the center of the universe
and that the earth was actually revolving around the sun. The full
force of the church came against this so-called heresy. The church
was embarrassed when proven wrong and perhaps too quickly embraced the scientific era of rationalism ushered in through the Enlightenment. This led to many good developments in discovery and
understanding, but along the way Scripture, theology and doctrine

were subjugated by the epistemology of the era. Theologians in the eighteenth and nineteenth centuries were convinced that by approaching the Bible according to the prevailing thinking of their day, they were actually protecting the integrity of Scripture and supporting the existence of God. But a modernist mindset wants to explain mystery instead of embrace it. In *A Future for Truth*, Henry H. Knight discusses William Placher's view of transcendence:

> The "domestication" of God's transcendence begins with Protestant and Roman Catholic scholasticism, which attempted in various ways to clearly and rationally explain what had previously been assumed to be beyond human explanation.[1]

Domesticating God's transcendence led to a Christianity that was safe and devoid of the radical nature of Christ's call to discipleship. Discussions of postmodernity create opportunities to rethink theology and perhaps free the living and sacred Word of God from the systematic rationalism of modernity. Scripture, theology and life are filled with paradox. Postmodern students have little problem living with paradox; they're more interested in seeking an encounter with a living and magnificent God. We must be aware of the opportunities and the dangers, however, employing wisdom to properly navigate through the turbulence of change.

> So many Christians have created a faith that fits into the American dream, a faith that is rarely challenged. I think many believe in Jesus because we, the church, portray Christianity as easy.
>
> **JUSTIN, COLLEGE STUDENT**

FAITH AND THIS GENERATION

The most extensive study of religion and youth ever done in the United States, the National Study of Youth and Religion (NSYR), has yielded a vast amount of information. Around 50 percent of adolescents claim that faith is important in their lives, influencing choices they make. Forty percent claim they practice their faith in meaningful ways on a daily basis. Most who say they are Christians attend church and youth ministry events. Yet by and large, these youth remain uninformed about established Christian beliefs. At the International Study for Youth Ministry Forum in London, Kenda Creasy Dean, a member of the NSYR research team, spoke about core attitudes and beliefs emerging among young people in our churches today:

- God wants people to be good, nice and fair to each other as taught in the Bible and by most world religions.
- The central goal of life is to be happy and to feel good about oneself.
- God does not need to be particularly involved in one's life except when God is needed to resolve a problem.
- Good people go to heaven when they die.[2]

> Jesus was radical, reaching out to those who had been forgotten. I think at times churches in North America could not possibly do a worse job at imitating Jesus. We are complacent, lukewarm and judgmental. We have watered down the message of the gospel in a dangerous way.
>
> **KRISTEN, 18 YEARS OLD**

Have we created a god in our own image, a god conveniently in line with our American lifestyle? Do we make ourselves feel that we are really sacrificing to serve this god by adhering to a list of a few cultural taboos that good Christians don't do, all the while ignoring the God who is calling us to be revolutionary kingdom people? The NSYR study indicates youth are embracing a moralistic therapeutic deism because that's what they are being taught in our churches. What they see is what they are becoming.

As youth workers we must allow the passion of kids to feed on the passion of Jesus' radical life and message. Adolescents will resonate with it if it is properly communicated to them. Early followers of Jesus turned the world upside down by proclaiming the radical message that Jesus is Lord, not Caesar, our nationalistic idealism, our political party or the American dream ideology. The call to follow this true God is not safe or convenient, unlike much of the feel-good, carefree god-think being modeled to our young people today. The presence of Jesus Christ in the lives of adolescents who are nurtured by the power of Scripture is not safe, but it's the essence of presence-centered youth ministry.

FOUR

A New Kind of Youth Worker

Fear—the fear of losing our Christian nation, the fear of popular culture, the fear of compromising truth, the fear of losing our kids, the fear of change, and on and on—is a major factor affecting how we engage in youth ministry today. The fear that keeps us from creating loving environments for youth ministry is the same fear that is a major factor in the actual departure of kids from the church.

We press for bigger and better events, more talented and cooler youth workers, and more effective strategies. We condemn popular culture so kids will better understand how bad it is for them. We emphasize hard-hitting chastity campaigns to insure our kids avoid sexual activity. We think we just have to be more convincing, work harder and communicate better; then we can turn this around.

Our churches are full of fear because the people in them are full of fear. Parents want youth workers and youth ministry programs that will fix their kids—modify their behavior. Parents hope that youth ministry will make their kids nice American citizens who think the right things and do the right things like sign virginity pledge cards and never take a drink of alcohol.

All this fear leads us to engage in youth ministry based on behavioral modification techniques and poisons the environment of genuine transformation, which comes only through the work of the Holy Spirit. Most parents think they want their kids to love and serve Jesus, but they don't want their kids to get too extreme. It can be scary if the Holy Spirit actually starts transforming kids. God might desire something from teenagers that their Christian parents don't approve of.

FOLLOWING GOD IS NOT SAFE

Carrie decided to work on our camp staff the summer after she graduated from college. Working with high school girls at camp she decided would be a good way to spend the summer before settling into her high paying new career with a large international corporation. Carrie was full of energy and extremely talented, so she enthusiastically embraced her role as a cabin leader. The girls in her cabin loved her.

Within a couple of weeks Carrie was starting to have second thoughts about her career choice. By the third week she asked me about the possibility of working in youth ministry. She said, "I love working with these girls and being in this community of God seekers." A week later she began expressing stronger doubts that she could go into the corporate world. "I just don't think I can be fulfilled sitting at a desk making money. I love mentoring the girls God brings me into relationship with." I reminded her that she had been in this role for only a month and that she needed to keep praying about it and take time to continue thinking about it. I told her that she had

> Do I think that Christians are serious about the message of Christ to deny ourselves, follow him and take care of the least of these? No, I don't. American culture is very self-centered and focused on what we can get out of life, not on helping others. The church is doing a better job imitating our culture than imitating Jesus.
>
> **LIZ, COLLEGE STUDENT**

experienced a month-long mountain-top experience and that youth ministry is also filled with a lot of valleys and disappointments. I didn't want her to make a hasty, emotional decision.

As the summer rolled on, her resolve to pursue youth ministry grew. Several days after she told her parents, I received a phone call from Carrie's dad requesting that I join her parents in a phone conference. During the call her parents explained they were Christians and actively involved in their church, but they were concerned about their daughter's intention to pursue youth ministry. "Carrie has just finished college and prepared for this wonderful job opportunity that will enable her to support herself and begin an exciting career. How will she support herself doing youth ministry? We think she's overreacting, and we want you to discourage her from doing this."

I could identify with their concern; I too have a daughter and know what it's like to want the best for her. Would I want Jessica, our twenty-year-old daughter, to walk away from the American dream and choose something that would be difficult? Thoughts flashed through my mind during the conversation. I thought about how I want my kids to follow the call of God in their lives, but what if Jessica announced that she was being called to a country in the developing world? How would I react? How would my wife react? To be honest, I think we would freak out. In the midst of this conference call, it was no longer just about Carrie and her parents. It was about me and my faith and my willingness to let God have my kids.

I shared with Carrie's parents—actually speaking to myself—that following God is not safe.

Responding to the call of Jesus in our lives may lead—in all likelihood does lead—to the opposite of conventional life plans. Carrie's parents stated that she could follow Jesus working at the job that was waiting for her. I explained that any job a Christian does should be viewed as ministry, and if God is calling Carrie to this job, she and they should view it as a calling, a vocation. On the other hand, if God was clearly calling Carrie to ministry, she should obey God rather than men, or even her parents.

I ended the conversation by asking them something that just popped into my mind (and believe me this was more the Holy Spirit speaking than me). "I wonder what Mother Teresa's parents said to her when she announced to them, 'Dad, Mom, I believe God is calling me to the poor who are dying of disease and poverty. They need someone to hold them as they die, to show them the dignity they deserve being created in the imago Dei. Oh, and Mom, Dad, I believe God wants me to do this in India.'"

Mother Teresa obviously had parents. I wonder how they responded to her calling. More than that, I wondered how I would have responded if I were her dad. Do we *really* want our kids to follow the call of God on their lives? In *The Signature of Jesus* Brennan Manning writes, "Today many churches attempt to eliminate the risk and danger of this call. We cushion the risk and remove the danger of discipleship by drawing up a list of moral rules that give us security instead of holy insecurity."[1] There is a lot of confusion about what it means to be in the world (culture) but not of the world (culture). The need to isolate teenagers from the world in order to protect them from evil leads to dysfunctional Christianity.

Christ is not against culture; Christ is against sin. He commands us to be salt and light within culture. This is not always easy to do, but the Bible and church history are filled with examples of young people who were used by God in amazing yet dangerous ways. Joseph, Josiah, Daniel, David and Mary, the mother of Jesus, are biblical evidence that God uses young people. Young Josiah reformed a nation. Young David defeated Goliath. Young Daniel attended pagan

Adolescents are looking for a soul-shaking, heart-waking, world-changing God to fall in love with, and if they do not find that God in the Christian church, they will most certainly settle for lesser gods elsewhere. Youth look to the church to show them something. Most of the time we have offered them pizza.

KENDA CREASY DEAN AND RON FOSTER IN *THE GODBEARING LIFE*

schools, where he was thrust into the academic disciplines of magic and false religions, and was hailed by the Babylonian intelligentsia as a rising star. He chose his battles wisely, ultimately causing a whole nation to consider God.

TEENS ARE FEARFUL TOO

To be fair, not just parents are anxious. Many young people in the church are also fearful. Some anxiety is normal adolescent insecurity, but much of the fear they experience has been nurtured by the church. Many of them have been discipled into a state of anxiety through behavior modification.

- I'm not sure I believe all the things my church believes.
- I have been told that a Christian doesn't think this way or do these things, so I can't be a real Christian.
- I violated my "True Love Waits" pledge card. I'm finished, God is through with me.
- I don't measure up.

The messages they may hear in response include

- You just need more faith.
- You aren't really serious about your faith.
- You have sin in your life.
- You love the world more than you love God.

Most of the time these thoughts aren't spoken overtly. But they're implied and reinforced through the environment we've created, so many kids who are just trying to figure out what is means to follow Jesus have been driven right out of the church.

Presence-centered ministry is about creating an environment where we and those around us are able to come face to face with God. We're allowed space to attend to God's presence. The story of Jesus acknowledging our primary need to sit at his feet to learn, to worship and to *be* is a seminal verse for me and for this book.

> Now as they went on their way, he entered a certain village, where a woman named Martha welcomed him into her home. She had a sister named Mary, who sat at the Lord's feet and listened to what he was saying. But Martha was distracted by her many tasks; so she came to him and asked, "Lord, do you not care that my sister has left me to do all the work by myself? Tell her then to help me." But the Lord answered her, "Martha, Martha, you are worried and distracted by many things; there is need of only one thing. Mary has chosen the better part, which will not be taken away from her. (Lk 10:38-42)

The presence of God manifests the love of God, exposing our anxieties and fears. Martha was full of worries and distractions. Mary, on the other hand, was at the feet of the Lord, having chosen the better way. More and more young people are ready to choose the better way.

> Finding a place of quiet and solitude for prayer has been my favorite part of the day hands down. It gives me time to slow down my day, focus on God and be in his presence, even if it's just for fifteen or twenty minutes. When I don't embrace this kind of rhythm, I miss out on the awareness of being in God's presence. Spending time with Jesus helps me remember what's important in life.
>
> **JESSICA, 17 YEARS OLD**

A REVOLUTION IN WAITING

In an interview with Homiletics Online, Robert Webber commented on the present state of youth ministry.

> Youth ministry is moving away from parties, picnics, *Fear Factor* kinds of things, to much more serious Bible study, prayer and things of that sort. I was at a Methodist conference in Pittsburgh, and the speaker was talking about youth ministry. He said he had tried everything in the book to get youth to come to the church: pizza parties, retreats, the whole thing. One day, he said, it was like God spoke to [him]: "You know, these kids have plenty of parties connected with school and so on." So [he] shut the whole thing down and just started a Friday night prayer meeting and Bible study. He said, "I've no room for all the kids that are coming. . . ."
>
> There is a new seriousness about young people, millennial people. They don't want to be entertained. They want to be challenged. They want a faith that is challenging as opposed to a Christianity that is entertaining.[2]

Gerald Celente, director of the Trends Research Institute calls these students *a revolution in waiting.* He says the Millennials (or postmodern generation) are the first generation since the Boomers to be activists. They'll respond to our coaching if we take the message of Christ seriously and present them with a big-picture plan of kingdom building.

Brennan Manning adds to this conversation:

> Unless the Church of the Lord Jesus creates a countercurrent to the drift of materialism, self-indulgence, and nationalism, Christians merely adapt to the secular environment in a tragic distortion of the gospel. The words of Jesus are reinterpreted to mean anything, everything, and nothing. One school of

thought, for example, assures us that the New Testament is filled with Oriental exaggerations, that Jesus never intended us to take the gospel literally. . . .

Such reductionisms dilute the radical demands of discipleship so that Jesus is frequently honored today for what he did not mean rather than for what he did mean.[3]

Teenagers see indifference in churches and conclude that we don't take the message of Jesus seriously. And yet I am encouraged that more and more young people are willing to take Jesus at his word and put it into practice. So many passionate young people are filled with enough ideology to actually believe that Jesus was serious about the things he said.

> I think some Christians take seriously the things Jesus said about what it means to follow him, but most dance around the message of Jesus, forgetting the whole serving-and-taking-care-of-the-poor-and-hungry part.
>
> **LAUREN, 15 YEARS OLD**

In *Practicing Passion: Youth and the Quest for a Passionate Church,* Kenda Creasy Dean shows how the church has used behavior modification techniques in a misguided attempt to accomplish spiritual transformation of youth. Dean focuses on the distinct adolescent life-stage attribute of passion. People in the church are so fearful of adolescent passion they go to extraordinary, nonbiblical efforts to tame it. Dean believes domesticating adolescent passion removes a God-given life force that not only works against individual transformation but also robs the church. The power to turn the world upside down comes when the church connects the passion of the adolescent with the passion of Christ.

When these two passions come together, the results are not necessarily nice, easy or safe, but they capture the imagination of young people who just might be willing to embrace Jesus' challenge: "Let them deny themselves and take up their cross and follow me. For those who want to save their life will lose it, and those who lose their life for my sake, and for the sake of the gospel, will save it" (Mk 8:34-35).

Dean points to the act of *mimesis* (from the Greek word that we translate "imitation") as the process through which we actually embody and enact what we're imitating. She writes:

The objective of the holy life is conformity to God in Jesus Christ, whose self-giving love enables our own. After all, what if young people actually do what Jesus does? What if an adolescent we know actually does identify with the God of the cross, and therefore does love something truly, with the kind of passion that exposes all lesser loves, including the greedy, self-fulfilling ones on which human society stands?

Mimesis of Jesus Christ does not create "good teenagers" or "wholesome youth programs." It creates radicals and prophets—people who reveal the root of cultural deceits with the searchlight of Christ's love, and who unmask avarice, violence, rivalry, and smallness, exposing them like the Wizard of Oz behind the curtain. And like the Wizard, the ideologies of self-fulfillment can no longer intimidate once the humbug has been revealed.[4]

DYING FOR A CAUSE

If we're willing to abandon ourselves to the radical cause of Christ, youth will join us. They are desperate for real life, something worth laying down their lives for. Teenagers (and adults for that matter) continue to flock to movie theaters, where they get a glimpse of what it might be like to live heroically. We're attracted to bigger-than-us life and adventure. Failing to connect the call of God to this inherent desire in human beings, we tinker with our generic invitations to be "good for God."

Presence-centered youth ministry focuses on the passionate narrative of Scripture and the priority of prayer to create space for youth to encounter the transformation of the Holy Spirit. Praying and meditating on Scripture naturally (and supernaturally) lead young people to acts of mercy and ultimately to justice. Today's young people who are following Jesus are increasingly troubled by the state of Christianity. Increasing numbers of them are refusing to follow the old script. They will not prop up the hypocrisy so prevalent in our churches. They want Jesus. They want to obey the Holy Spirit. They want to honor God. Here are some examples I've seen lately:

> If you look at the New Testament, the message of Jesus is exciting, dangerous and life changing; today the message of Jesus and living a life following him is not very different than living without him.
>
> **LAURA, COLLEGE STUDENT**

- Lindsay, a high school senior who has been a regular at Youth-Front camps and mission trips, shared with me her concern for providing services that senior citizens might need beyond Meals on Wheels. She felt God spoke to her to develop a ministry to run errands, pick up groceries and provide other help for senior citizens. Her efforts have been so successful she is forming a not-for-profit organization to carry on this much-needed ministry.

- Three high school guys from an affluent community shared ideas on how to be free from the consumerist environment they lived in.

- Teenagers completed two houses at the YouthFront mission

site in Croc, Mexico, and dedicated them to the Mexican families who would live in them. I wept as they presented one of them to Maria, a widow with seven children. It was a real-life example of caring for orphans and widows in their distress (Jas 1:27).

- Young people at Rock the Light, a music festival hosted by YouthFront, gave nearly $25,000 for victims of Hurricane Katrina. Teams of teenagers mobilized to assist in the disaster relief.

Colleen Carroll, a *St. Louis Post Dispatch* editor, has written a best-selling book called *The New Faithful* in which she documents the return of young adults to Christian basics and deeper commitment. She won a fellowship that allowed her a year to study the religious life of late adolescents. Her findings are quite amazing:

In evangelical circles, young adults often recall many sermons on personal salvation but few discussions of how Christians should treat the poor, engage the culture, or learn from Christian history and tradition. They complain of pastors focused more on winning converts than helping the converted live out their Christian faith and of worship leaders more interested in entertaining the congregation than encouraging reverence for God.[5]

Listed is a summary of the key characteristics she discovered of late-adolescent attitudes toward religion and the practices they are embracing.

- Their identity is centered on their religious beliefs, and their morality derives from those beliefs.
- They are attracted to the worldview that challenges many core values of the dominant secular culture while addressing their

deepest questions and concerns. Time-tested teachings and meaningful traditions appeal to them.

- They embrace challenging faith commitments that offer them firm guidelines on how to live.

- Their adherence to traditional morality and religious devotion often comes at considerable personal cost. The sacrificial nature of these commitments is precisely what makes them attractive.

- These teens yearn for mystery and tend to trust their intuitive sense that what they have found is true, real and worth living to the extreme.

- They seek guidance from legitimate sources of authority and trust these authorities to help them find lasting happiness and avoid repeating their own painful mistakes or those of their parents and peers.

- They strive for personal holiness, authenticity and integration in their spiritual lives and are attracted to people who do the same. Conversely, they are repelled by complacency, hypocrisy and pandering.

- Their beliefs and practices—though compatible with the core tenets of their faith traditions—often defy conventional wisdom about their generation, the expectations of religious leaders and existing classifications of believers within individual denominations (for example, charismatic or conventional, liberal or conservative).

- They are for the most part concerned with impacting and engaging the larger culture. Yet they are equally committed to living out their beliefs in the context of authentic communities that support them and hold them accountable.

Carroll's findings resonate with my experiences among young people. Notice her statement that young people are seeking guidance and formation from trusted authority figures. This sounds like the basis of a new kind of youth ministry.

The Youth Worker as Spiritual Guide

What do youth want from youth workers? Men and women who love Jesus and live what they believe, whose main "boast" is that they understand and know God. Presence-centered youth ministry starts with youth workers who practice the presence of God.

According to Brother Lawrence, the seventeenth-century author of *The Practice of the Presence of God*, the primary job of all Christians—young and old—is to commune with God, to place themselves in the presence of God. That's all. Brother Lawrence writes, "We cannot avoid the dangers and reefs that life holds without the very present help of God. . . . How can we ask for it unless we are with Him? How can we think often about Him except through the holy practice that we must form within ourselves?"[1] He proposed a holistic approach

> Thus says the LORD: Do not let the wise boast in their wisdom, do not let the mighty boast in their might, do not let the wealthy boast in their wealth; but let those who boast boast in this, that they understand and know me, that I am the LORD.
>
> **JEREMIAH 9:23-24**

to practicing the presence of God and acknowledging God in a variety of ways. He suggests that Christians consistently offer their heart to God throughout the day in small and mundane ways as well as big and

> The most important thing that a youth pastor can do in youth ministry is to continue to grow personally in his or her relationship with God. Relationships are so important for a successful ministry with youth, a relationship with God first and relationships with others second.
>
> **JOSH, COLLEGE STUDENT**

significant ways. At the time of Brother Lawrence's death, his abbot wrote, "We can judge the love that Lawrence had for his neighbor by his love for God. He was persuaded from what our Lord said in the Gospels, that the smallest service rendered to the least of our brothers is counted as done to God Himself."[2] Young people need youth workers who have God—rather than youth ministry—first and foremost in view.

I awakened shortly after the beginning of this new millennium to the reality that the church in general and youth ministry in particular were going to go through major corrections. Along with a plethora of new books on the emerging religious trends of adolescents, *Christianity Today, Group Magazine* and *Youth-Worker Journal* consistently carry articles documenting the craving of young people for orthodox Christianity, worship filled with transcendent encounters with God and a fascination with tradition. Robert Webber writes about this trend:

> The current change in worship taste and style is indeed a reflection of our shift into a postmodern world. The culture of post-2000 is very different than that of the sixties and seventies. It is a culture tired of noise, turned off by phoniness, sick of glitz, and wary of the superficial. It is a culture searching for an authentic encounter with God, longing for depth and substance, craving quiet and spiritual contemplation and moved by visual, tactile forms of communication. . . .
>
> They are much more likely to utilize liturgical elements than

their predecessors. And they reject slick, tightly orchestrated programs that are more show than "real." The younger evangelicals are "longing for an encounter with God's presence."[3]

Most of the time I'm speaking to youth workers these days, but last summer I had the privilege of speaking to high school students at a YouthFront camp after a two-year hiatus. I approached this week of speaking differently than I had in the past when I felt burdened to cover every area of teenage life—home life, friends, dating, peer pressure, commitment, entertainment and so on—like it was my responsibility to fix it all (in partnership with the Holy Spirit of course).

My desire this time was for one thing: to facilitate an encounter with the presence of God. I went into this week certain that the Holy Spirit didn't need my oratorical abilities or any other youth ministry talent I might have to transform the lives of young people. We read Scripture, shared stories, prayed, worshiped and sought the face of God. God showed up, Jesus was glorified, and the Holy Spirit changed lives. Spiritual transformation took place. Courtney, one of the teenagers present, wrote this:

> The most amazing thing this week was Wednesday night—the lights were all down—it was so emotional, when we sing I usually don't get emotional . . . but that night—it was like, I can't get enough of this. It was the mood—like no one was clapping and getting all worked up, you could sit down and seriously think about the words we were saying, and take them to heart, and you could actually mean what you were saying. Some people raise their hand. . . . I like to get down to the ground and pray.

I am convinced that students don't just want games, slick programs and entertainment, they want to encounter God. They want authenticity. They long to know and experience Christ and embrace something that calls them to a sacrificial challenge. I agree with Courtney, "I think God had a really good time that night."

MYSTERY OF THE DIVINE

Modern rationalism tells us that what's real can be verified scientifically. My early Christian training emphasized that experience was not important. The only experience that had validity was an experience that could be repeated in controlled environments. There had to be a level of certainty concerning the nature and dynamics of the experience. There was little room for metaphysical reality. This mindset submitted to scientific rationalism and conformed Christian practice to the prevailing ideology of the day.

Today modernity and its centuries-old embrace of scientific rationalism and assumed certainty has given way to quantum physics and the reemergence of metaphysical possibility. There is a new openness, even among the intelligentsia, to the mystery of the cosmos and an awareness that something amazing and unfathomable is occurring in the universe. In churches that have become cognitive-centric, the reemergence of a more holistic way to encounter God and the truth of God is a much-needed corrective. Young people want, even expect, to encounter the mystery of the divine. If someone tells young people they can have a relationship with God, experience better be connected to it.

Presence-centered youth ministry nurtures environments and opportunities for our young people to come face to face with God, which leads to transformation. And transformation that occurs in the lives of young people can't even be compared to the best behavior modification techniques. Recently a group of college students in Kansas City came together to start a worship gathering. They sent representatives to scope out possible spaces that would be conducive to worshiping God. They rejected space after space because, well, they were blah. When they went into an Orthodox church filled with icons, candles and other art, they agreed they had found the place that met their aesthetic needs.

Presence-centered youth ministry is about a radical realignment away from our doings—our programs, our expertise, our communication skills—to a focus on being: being real, being with God, being wrapped up in love with Jesus. Paul Gauche, the youth minister at Prince of Peace Lutheran Church in Burnsville, Minnesota, writes,

> The best thing my youth pastor did for us was to make his own personal walk with Jesus radical through prayer, fasting, worship, and intercession. Seeing him live extravagantly for God, set aside the pleasures of worldliness, live a simple life and make a zealous love for God his full-time job helped me enter into my own passionate love relationship with Christ.
>
> **LAURA, COLLEGE STUDENT**

> Our high-tech, hands-on, visually stimulating, hooked-up, wired-for-sound culture no longer provides what young people desire spiritually. Young people want to meet the mystery and majesty of a powerful God in candles and quiet instead of large-screen entertainment. They want to meet God by holding hands in prayer instead of down-loaded Bible studies synched to their Palm Pilots.[4]

PRACTICING THE PRESENCE OF GOD

To be a spiritual guide for youth and create a presence-centered youth ministry means youth workers must live, minister, guide, lead and mentor out of the wholeness of their souls. Youth workers who are effective spiritual guides are regularly in the presence of God.

> Youth pastors must make God the center of everything they do. The messages of youth pastors should [be] more about God's love and grace, not just what we shouldn't be doing. We also need to hear more about Jesus' words and life and how that impacts us today.
>
> **AMY, 14 YEARS OLD**

I'm enthusiastic about theological training and plan to be a student formally and informally for the rest of my life. More youth workers are being theologically trained to do ministry than ever before. They are learning systematic theology, hermeneutical skills, and other wonderful theological necessities. But many seminaries are failing to truly prepare and spiritually form men and women of God for ministry. Richard John Neuhaus underscored the need for theological training to embrace the students' spiritual formation rather than focusing almost exclusively on their religious education:

> What is needed is not the training of religious technicians but the formation of spiritual leaders. It is important for seminaries to impart skills and competencies; it is more important to ignite conviction and courage to lead. The language of facilitation is cool and low risk. The language of priesthood and prophecy and the pursuit of holiness is impassioned and perilous.[5]

> It is very important for youth pastors to make sure they are seeking God, being obedient to him and walking in the Spirit. We need youth leaders who are willing to take risks, try new things and take a step forward in their groups so they don't get stuck doing everything by habit, which leads to being mediocre.
>
> **TATE, COLLEGE STUDENT**

Programs are an important part of youth ministry if they are only the tip of the iceberg. The tip is always easy to see, beautiful, even massive, yet this part of the iceberg would not be evident but for the enormous mountain beneath the surface. The submerged part of a youth ministry should look quite different— quiet, compelling, deep. The submerged part of youth ministry is about youth workers' personal devotion and love for Jesus, about exploring ways to more dramatically fulfill the calling of youth ministry, and about praying and working for this vision to the glory of God.

A spiritual guide for youth is infected, consumed and fixated with Jesus. Os Guinness was asked by a non-Christian foreigner, "How come when I meet a Buddhist leader I feel like I am in the presence of a holy man, but when I meet a Christian leader, I feel like I have met an entrepreneur, a mover and shaker, a wheeler dealer?"[6] What a sad commentary on Christian leadership. Youth workers must ask themselves whether they are worth following, whether their lives are consistent with their words. French philosopher Maurice Blondel was fond of saying, "If you really want to understand what a man believes, don't listen to what he says, but watch what he does."

TRAVELING COMPANIONS

Are you worth watching? I'm not asking if you have it all together. The youth you work with are spiritually formed as much by watching you in your weaknesses as they are in seeing your strengths. Being a spiritual guide to youth means taking them with you on your journey and allowing them to be a part of your pilgrimage, just as you are on their journey with them.

One of my favorite icons is called *Christ and Saint Menas,* though I call it *Traveling Companions*. It's a Coptic icon painted in the eighth century in a monastery in upper Egypt where Menas served as abbot. It depicts Christ standing beside Menas, supporting and protecting him, and for me, inviting Menas to a lifelong friendship and journey together. It's a wonderful reminder of Christ's constant presence with us and of how we should view Christian formation with the youth whom God brings into our lives.

Jesus did not meet with his disciples once a week, so why do we relegate discipleship to some formal thing? The most beneficial aspect of youth ministry is for a minister to do life, all areas of it, with his or her students.

MOE, COLLEGE STUDENT

This icon has become quite meaningful to me, because it communicates in one picture what I am communicating in this entire book. Sharing the good news isn't a declaration from people who have all the answers and have appropriated all that the gospel conveys. Rather we share as much about God as we have come to understand, and we invite others to join us in our pilgrimage through life.

Youth ministry is about being with youth, not just as a role model or friend but also as a spiritual guide and a traveling companion. They need someone who will enter into a sacramental relationship with them and someone who will listen to them. They want compassionate listening, which is desperately needed in our churches.

Of course no one can personally relate to a hundred teenagers in this way; the whole congregation needs to be involved in the lives of the youth. One of the most important responsibilities youth workers have is to cast the vision for others in their congregation to join in the Christian formation of youth. They have to be able to communicate the importance of having passionate adults in the lives of adolescents. After communicating the reality of what is happening to youth who are walking away from the church, youth workers can invite others to pray a simple prayer: "God, should I be involved in the Christian formation of our youth?" They should be encouraged to fast for a time while praying about what role they might have. If after a time of prayer the adult does not feel compelled to get involved with the youth ministry, let them know that you are OK with them not accepting the invitation. Trying to manipulate others into involvement doesn't work; youth ministry is a calling. Every youth ministry needs adults who feel called.

Youth workers as spiritual guides will resist being so consumed with planning and executing programs that they can't guide youth. The way of the kingdom is through relationships, not events. Youth workers who serve as spiritual guides for youth nurture a presence-centered youth ministry by engaging in the hard work of creating an environment of authentic community. Successful youth ministries highly value having a deeply caring, safe community. Brennan Manning notes the importance of relationship in spiritual formation.

Paschal says that the truest test of discipleship is the way we live with each other in the community of faith. It is as simple and as demanding as that. In our words and deeds, we give shape and form to our faith every day. We make people a little better or leave them a little worse. We either affirm or deprive, enlarge or diminish the lives of others.[7]

Creating an environment of intimate community requires a new definition of success. I talk with youth pastors all over North America who know their performance is evaluated in terms of parental happiness and the number of students attending events. Without a doubt, counting the number of people attending is a more concrete endeavor than measuring intangible dynamics like authenticity, trust or spiritual maturity. The difficulty, as Eddie Gibbs states it, is this:

Measuring results in terms of increased attendance at worship services and other church-related activities creates a premature sense of achievement. We always have to ask who the new people are and where they are coming from. Is one church winning people simply at the expense of other congregations that do not have the resources to compete on equal terms in the religious marketplace?[8]

Having a youth pastor who really loved the Lord more than anything else and poured into me had a huge impact on my relationship with God. My youth pastor also helped me to understand what Christians past and present believe about the deep things of our faith. I actually began to understand, and it changed the way I loved and thought about the Lord.

KRISTEN, 18 YEARS OLD

How foolish to conclude that increasing numbers in a church or youth group correlates with spiritual growth and vitality.

AUTHENTICITY

A spiritual guide creates an atmosphere of authenticity. In *The Life You've Always Wanted,* John Ortberg tells the story of a little boy who went to Sunday school where he knew the sort of answers he was expected to give to the teacher's questions. The teacher asked, "What is brown and furry, has a long tail, and stores up nuts for winter?"

"Well," the boy muttered. "I guess the answer is Jesus, but it sure sounds like a squirrel to me."

Obviously the little guy's teacher created an environment with certain expectations about what to say and do. When we engage in behavior modification techniques to achieve certain results, we nurture environments of hypocrisy and deception, training young people to pretend to be spiritual and to give the "right" answers regardless of what they really think. We leave little room for openness and honesty.

Youth workers need to not be afraid to challenge kids. They need to speak truth.

EMILY, COLLEGE STUDENT

In *ChurchNext,* author Eddie Gibbs has much to say about what young people want in a church. "Polished performances and impeccable images turn them off. [Research] reminds us that they are suspicious of bigness, of advertising and ego trips. They want something: churches that are down-to-earth and unpretentious."[9]

Posing as people who have our act together is a formula for disaster when we want to connect intimately with today's youth.

This is not a generation seeking answers to the philosophical questions that have preoccupied Christian apologists. . . . They want to meet people who have a transforming relationship with God. [They] want to see individuals who demonstrate God-inspired service to their fellow human beings. They are attracted to people who are prepared to speak the truth whatever the personal cost. They respect honest people who are prepared to admit that there are things they don't understand as well as to own up to their own shortcomings.[10]

> If a youth ministry is genuine, uplifting and results in growth in one's spiritual journey, others will come. Youth ministry should not be about numbers. It's about Jesus.
>
> **JAMIE, COLLEGE STUDENT**

A PLACE FOR DOUBT

How do we go about creating an atmosphere of authenticity? We must first be open and honest. This sets the example that young people can tell the truth and share their opinions even when they know it's not the party line. We also encourage young people to ask questions and refuse to make up answers when none exist. We respect each other even when we don't see eye to eye. Entirely too often, the church ostracizes young people by being judgmental about their opinions, beliefs and behavior. An important aspect of nurturing authenticity is making sure the group is a safe place to express doubt. Jesus modeled this in the last chapter of Matthew when he met with his disciples after his resurrection.

The eleven disciples went to Galilee, to the mountain to which Jesus had directed them. When they saw him, they worshiped him; but some doubted. And Jesus came and said to them, "All authority in heaven and on earth has been given to me. Go therefore and make disciples of all nations, baptizing them in the name of the Father and of the Son and of the Holy Spirit, and teaching them to obey everything that I have commanded you. And remember, I am with you always, to the end of the age." (Mt 28:16-20)

His disciples had been with him for more than three years. They were with him when he raised people from the dead, walked on the water, and cast out demons. They heard his teaching and examined his life, so they worshiped him; but some doubted. *Some doubted.* We aren't told how many or who, just that some doubted. This is extraordinary.

Even more extraordinary is Jesus' response to their doubts. He didn't say, "OK, that is it. I've had enough! You saw all the things I've done. You heard all the things I've said. You saw me crucified, dead and buried, and now I'm here with you. You don't get it. What do I have to do to get through to you? Just forget it. I'm finished with you. Good riddance!" Instead Jesus commissioned them to make disciples. How can we be any less patient and gracious?

> A lot of kids have bad church experiences. There are so many broken people who dress up and hide their flaws and ridicule every one else whose mistakes surface. People are sick of the lack of authenticity.
>
> **MARK, COLLEGE STUDENT**

David had an honest, intense relationship with God. The Bible calls him a man after God's own heart even though he was a bloody soldier, a murderer, and an adulterer. What was it about David that made him a man after God's own heart? He would come into the presence of God with no pretense. David conversed with God intimately, never masking his emotions or managing his image before

God. David spoke passionately with God "How long are you going to let this go on? Why are you doing this?" God never reprimands David for being authentic.

Too often, standing between God and people who want to be real with God is a person who says, "You can't talk to God like that. You can't have doubt. Doubt is bad. Everything is wonderful." But we really know better and so do our young people. We're messed up. Many things are not as they should be. What we've been told by people we trusted isn't true. We know it, our youth know it, and God knows it.

AN HONEST CRY TO GOD

A lot of Christians were uncomfortable with the movie *Saved,* but during the first thirty minutes of the movie I was having a hearty laugh. It presented an excellent satire on Christian subculture, spoofing many things I've done myself. Though I didn't particularly like how the movie ended, one scene was so powerful it moved me to tears.

Jena Malone portrays Mary, a Christian girl in the Christian school. Mary used to be in the in crowd of "good Christians." Mary makes some bad, misinformed choices and ends up pregnant. She feels forgotten by God. As the burden of her situation weighs heavily on her, Mary approaches a large statue of Jesus. Mary screams obscenities at the statue. I'm not saying we should encourage our kids to pray like this, but we'd better recognize a sincere prayer—an honest cry to God—when we see it.

> If young people live off of what they are told to believe rather than experiencing faith themselves they will not stay connected to church.
>
> **TATE, COLLEGE STUDENT**

Part of the emotion of this scene for me was remembering a similar situation when I was a senior in high school. I dedicated my high school years to swimming. I wanted to excel. I trained in the pool every day for hours. I broke school records, got media coverage and was accepted into the elite athletes clique. What I wanted was state recognition and a scholarship. In one of the most important swim meets, however, I failed to achieve a major goal. I was crushed.

This happened shortly after I decided to pursue a relationship with God. I remember driving down the highway near my home and feeling enraged with anger and disappointment. I started beating the dashboard of my car and screaming at the top of my lungs. Through tears of anger I cursed God. I blamed God. I called God names. I asked God *why*.

Suddenly I felt the presence of God in my car. I remember thinking, *God is going to kill me*. I felt convicted, then forgiven and loved. I had God's full attention, and he entered into my frustration and disappointment. It was a turning point in my Christian faith.

DOUBT AND FAITH

We see many examples in Scripture of people speaking honestly with God, expressing doubts and even arguing and questioning their plight.

> You have made us like sheep for slaughter, and have scattered us among the nations. You have sold your people for a trifle, demanding no high price for them. . . . Rouse yourself! Why do you sleep, O Lord? Awake, do not cast us off forever! Why do you hide your face? Why do you forget our affliction and oppression? (Ps 44:11-12, 23-24)

God looks all over the world for people who will converse with him in honest dialogue, who will come before him doubts and all.

Many autobiographies of great Christians contain the theme of doubt as a part of their spiritual process, and many great thinkers have given credence to doubt:

> If we begin with certainties, we shall end in doubts; but if we begin with doubts, and we are patient in them, we shall end in certainties. (Sir Francis Bacon)

> It is not as a child that I believe and confess Jesus Christ. My hosanna is born of a furnace of doubt. (Fyodor Dostoyevsky, author, *The Brothers Karamazov*)

> Faith which does not doubt is dead faith. (Miguel de Unamuno, philosopher and novelist)

> Be patient toward all that is unsolved in your heart. And try to love the questions themselves. (Rainer Maria Rilke, twentieth-century poet)

> Whether your faith is that there is a God or that there is not a God, if you don't have any doubts you are either kidding yourself or asleep. Doubts are the ants in the pants of faith. They keep it awake and moving. (Frederick Buechner, author, *Wishful Thinking*)

It makes sense to allow teenagers a place to deconstruct their faith and figure out what they believe about Jesus Christ and being his follower, since it isn't better for them to figure it out after they leave the youth group. Is it any wonder that more than 80 percent of kids drop out of church once they get to college? We haven't prepared them to own their faith. And by preparing them I don't mean filling their heads with more evidence that demands a verdict. I mean helping them to discover a real faith that goes beyond good behavior and the verbal assent to doctrinal statements. Josh, a college student, acknowledges this delicate balance:

> Growing up in the church, we depend a lot on our parents, youth pastor and pastor's faith to base our relationships with God. For most teenagers, everything we know about faith is based on what we are told. We need other people's help but we also need to build and own our own faith.

MINISTERING FROM OUR FULLNESS

How can we be effective as a pastor to youth unless we minister to youth out of the overflow of a life with God? We need to insist that Christian formation practices, such as a periodic personal spiritual retreat, are actually in our job descriptions.

Many youth pastors also have job descriptions that require ministry to be conducted within the four walls of the church. One youth pastor told me how a church administrator "caught" him in his office one day. The administrator stressed how happy he was to have him there. Thinking he was appreciated for being on the church staff, the youth pastor responded, "I'm glad I'm here also."

The church administrator clarified his statement by saying, "No, I mean I'm literally glad to see you here in your office working," insinuating he must not be working much.

The youth pastor responded by asking, "What does the title on my office door say?"

The church administrator replied, "Youth pastor."

To this the youth pastor asked, "Do you see any youth in here?"

The point, hopefully, was well taken.

So how do we nurture a presence-centered youth ministry that values ushering youth into the presence of God? How do we walk faithfully as women and men of God who are serving as spiritual guides to youth? How do we encourage youth to join us as spiritual traveling companions? The answer may seem overly simplistic, but the only way to accomplish these things is to be people who passionately pursue the presence of God, who spend time at the feet of Jesus, and who intensely engage in our own Christian formation through spiritual practices.

> Youth pastors should become less concerned with the image of their youth ministries and the numbers of kids who show up and who come for an altar call and focus more of their energy on loving kids where they're at. I think God desires to do huge things through our generation. We need youth pastors who challenge us and teach solid, biblical truth.
>
> **KRISTEN, 18 YEARS OLD**

Seraphim of Sarov is the most revered Russian Orthodox saint. Seraphim was a monk who lived from 1759 to 1833, primarily in and around a monastery located in Sarov, Russia, southeast of Moscow. He's known for seeking the presence of God through a life of solitude. At one point he lived for sixteen years in a secluded hermitage in the woods outside of the monastery at Sarov. He came out of seclusion only to discern that his departure had been premature. He went into seclusion for another five years. When Seraphim of Sarov finally sensed the Holy Spirit leading him out, he received pilgrims seeking spiritual guidance. More than two thousand people lined up to see him on some days.

His ministry of spiritual direction, healing and miracles was quite extraordinary. Commonly people who met him expressed that they had experienced an overwhelming sense of God's presence while in the company of this godly man. Though some might criticize him for being so heavenly minded that he was no earthly good, he lived for face-to-face communion with God. Seraphim's motivation is amazing and powerful: "Learn to be at peace, and thousands all around you will be saved."[11]

We would be wise to take a deep breath and contemplate these words and the impact they could make on our ministries if we too found peace through an intimate relationship with God. Maybe we can't live in solitude for twenty-one years, but spending time in solitude at the feet of Jesus, meditating on Scripture, praying and listening for the still, small voice of the Holy Spirit will deepen our life with God.

A youth worker must be committed to a living and real life with God—not only as a follower of Christ but also as a youth minister. I highly recommend that you speak to your church leadership about writing into your job description a consistent rhythm of time and experiences devoted to cultivating your life with God. Psalm 78 speaks of David being called by God to shepherd God's people. "With upright heart he tended them, and guided them with skillful hand" (Psalm 78:72). Upright hearts and skillful hands are developed in the furnace of solitude, devotion and communion with God. This should be your testimony.

AUTHENTIC TESTIMONIES

Revelation 12 describes a great spiritual war between the forces of good and evil. Those who are conquerors are described in verse 11:

> People working with youth need to be completely real: real as a person, real about life, and real with the Bible. Jesus didn't sugarcoat things.
>
> **KYLE, COLLEGE STUDENT**

"But they have conquered him by the blood of the Lamb and by the word of their testimony for they did not cling to life even in the face of death." Most of us have an understanding of "the blood of the Lamb," but what about "the word of their testimony"? How does the word of our testimony make us conquerors?

Often when we think of *testimony*, what comes to mind is telling a conversion experience. In this context, however, testimony is the present reality of God at work in our lives. To help us articulate our testimonies, we can ask ourselves questions like these:

- What is God showing me today—not ten years ago, but today?
- What is God teaching me this week?
- What has God been convicting me of recently?
- How is God at work in my life now?

Stop and think about your testimony. How would you answer these questions? Do you have an ongoing testimony?

When we seek to be spiritual guides, we desire to be in the presence of God, to maintain a testimony of relationship with God, to nurture our personal spirituality and wholeness of soul. The youth we work with are drawn to authentic and active testimony, not to a Hollywood production. They want to know we love God and that we believe the stuff we talk about. Our knowledge and experience mean little if we aren't regularly experiencing the love of Christ. I would even say knowledge and experience can actually make us detrimental to the purposes of God if we aren't practicing the presence of God.

When we consider that God is in and among us, and that in God we live and move and have our being, then it's reasonable to conclude that we can practice the presence of God without ceasing, alone and in the company of those we do life with. Living a life attentive to the presence of God will create an environment that helps the adolescents we work with to recognize God at work in their lives as well. We cultivate our own ongoing testimony, nurture the fullness of our own spirit and submit ourselves to be the spiritual guides we are called to be as youth ministers when we stay tuned into the presence of God in our world. We serve each other by reminding one another that God is present and available for each encounter with us.

SIX

Trusting the Holy Spirit with Your Ministry

I distinctly remember the overwhelming sense of being in sacred space from the moment I stepped foot in Taizé, a Christian community located in southern France, near the historic city of Cluny, which was itself a center of renewed spirituality during the medieval period.

In 1940, Brother Roger, the founder of the Taizé community, left his home in Switzerland to pursue his vision of establishing a community where God would be glorified and the gospel lived out through an ethos of simplicity, hospitality and reconciliation. The Holy Spirit led Brother Roger to the simple village of Taizé, where a few villagers welcomed him with warm hospitality. The tensions of World War II were building in Europe as Hitler sought to advance his empire. During the war Brother Roger offered assistance to fleeing refugees, including Jews who were trying to avoid Nazi concentration camps.

After the war Taizé became known as a place of peace—peace on earth and peace with God. By the early 1960s, larger and larger groups of young people flocked to Taizé. Currently young people between the ages of sixteen and twenty-six come year round to spend a week entering into the rhythm of prayer, solitude and the pursuit of

God's presence. During the months of warm weather as many as six thousand young people per week arrive from all over the world.

When we arrived, my friend Ronnie and I looked at each other, speechless, aware that God's presence was evident. We were in the midst of nearly five thousand young people who had all come to spend a week living in community with more than a hundred brothers who had pledged themselves to a life of prayer, worship, simplicity, reconciliation and justice. The brothers come from more than two dozen countries and a variety of Protestant and Catholic backgrounds to live together in a way that offers the hope of reconciliation among all people.

I was overwhelmed by the number of young people who come to Taizé, searching for meaning and an encounter with God. They don't come for contemporary, relevant worship experiences. In fact, the rhythm of Taizé revolves around three one-hour prayer times per day when the entire community comes together to pray, sing contemplative melodic Scripture songs, sit for long periods of silence and listen to Scripture readings. People also have the option of spending the entire week in silence. Everyone in the community helps with cleaning, preparing meals, washing dishes and other tasks. During the afternoons, group meetings allow people to explore topics such as forgiveness, responding to God's call and living for God in a pluralistic world. As I experienced Taizé for myself and observed a group of young people going through their week, I was awestruck by the transformation that occurred before me.

I was also aware that the brothers weren't in a frenzy to address every area of adolescent life. They gave no instruction on whom to date, when to date, how far is too far, what kind of music to listen to and so on. They didn't pressure the young people to make particular decisions. They focused on leading them into the presence of God, exposing them to Scripture, creating space for them to listen to the Holy Spirit and nurturing prayer. The brothers let the Holy Spirit work transformation and bring salvation. They trusted the Holy Spirit in a way that acknowledged God is in control.

GOD GIVES THE GROWTH

Too often, we depend on our training, gifts and abilities to accomplish the results we want to see in our ministries and the lives of the youth we work with. In presence-centered youth ministry, we trust the Holy Spirit. Scripture reminds us that though we participate, supernatural transformation is the result of the Holy Spirit's work:

> What then is Apollos? What is Paul? Servants through whom you came to believe, as the Lord assigned to each. I planted, Apollos watered, but God gave the growth. So neither the one who plants nor the one who waters is anything, but only God who gives the growth. (1 Cor 3:5-7)

When we push young people to make decisions, when we use behavior modification techniques to pressure youth to think certain thoughts and behave in "Christian" ways, *we* assume the role of the Holy Spirit. The problem is these practices don't lead to genuine transformation, and ultimately they do more harm than good.

I don't believe a single youth worker would defend a youth ministry philosophy that intentionally states behavior modification techniques as a viable practice. You won't see a youth ministry book titled *Behavior Mod-Driven Youth Ministry.* So why do we continue to act as if it is up to us to transform our youth? Why do we have difficulty living as if it's up to the Holy Spirit to transform them? The answer is because we're consistently evaluated in ways that pressure us to take results into our own hands. We're expected to have the "right kind" of kids in the youth group. We're expected to make our youth so spiritually mature that they don't get into trouble at school. We're paid to be so intellectually stimulating when we teach the Bible that our youth get good grades in school. We must model such great marriage relationships that youth wait until they're in the final stages of their education before they begin dating.

Of course I'm being sarcastic, but we're expected to accomplish something with a young person that even their parents are unable to do. These kinds of unscriptural expectations lead to dysfunction and get in the way of genuine transformation that comes only when a young person, through the Holy Spirit, comes face to face with our great God.

Nevertheless we can facilitate the process by nurturing an environment in which youth can be exposed to the presence of God all the while remembering the Holy Spirit works in a way we can't formalize into a technique or program. "Do not be astonished that I said to you, 'You must be born from above.' The wind blows where it chooses, and you hear the sound of it, but you do not know where it comes from or where it goes. So it is with everyone who is born of the Spirit" (Jn 3:7-8). How many combinations of the wind blowing are there? When you take into account velocity, direction, patterns and temperature, the combinations are endless. Likewise, all stories of personal salvation and transformation are unique because we have a creative God.

THE HOLY SPIRIT'S TIMING

Trusting the Holy Spirit in our ministries is not always easy. Marilyn Lazlo, a linguist who spent years as a Wycliffe missionary in Papua New Guinea among a tribe that had no written language and had never seen a white person, tells this story that illustrates this point.

Marilyn discovered soon after her arrival that the tribe had a social system revolving around polygamy. She desperately wanted to point them to a better way, to the scriptural way, but the Holy Spirit instructed her to remain silent. Marilyn went about her work of learning the language, creating an alphabet, teaching the villagers to read and write, and translating the Scriptures into this newly written language, all the while remaining silent on polygamy for more than fifteen years even though many had become Christians.

Even after the villagers enthusiastically received the Scripture in their own language, Marilyn didn't direct them to verses dealing with polygamy. She watched and trusted the work of the Holy Spirit. It took another eighteen months for the village leaders to discover for themselves through Scripture that they had a problem with their social and economic framework. They responded to Scripture and resolved the issue on their own so that the village has no polygamy now. Marilyn reflects, "If I had done it my way, they probably would have roasted me over an open fire!"

I'm much less patient than Marilyn, so I'm often tempted to take the spiritual development of a young person into my own hands. It requires intense faith to trust that the Holy Spirit is fully in control of transformation. Which of the following scenarios would you rather live in?

- You're well equipped to challenge and convince youth to live a mature Christian life. You accomplish this through great programming and powerful messages. You've constructed an environment where positive peer pressure creates an atmosphere where non-Christian behavior is looked down on so that righteous behavior prevails among your youth. The parents are happy; the deacons are happy; the pastor is happy. Life is good.

A youth worker magazine is planning to profile you and your ministry as a model for other youth workers. Inside you wonder if it's all real.

• You're convinced you'll have to be patient and lead youth on a path of Christian formation so they own their faith. You know they have serious questions about the Christian faith that you're not willing to ignore, but you allow them to live in their doubts, protecting their discovery process. You stand by adolescents who have made huge mistakes. The youth group is nothing like it was when the previous youth pastor (hired by a bigger church), was running it, and you know people are comparing you with him. You sense, however, that the Holy Spirit is at work in the lives of many of the young people.

Of course these scenarios are oversimplified, but most of us know that the spiritual choice is the second scenario, even though the first scenario seems more measurable and successful. We know that it wouldn't be long before the second scenario would lead to confrontations with parents and church leaders. Conflict would occur even if we could somehow prove that the second scenario would result in a 30 percent increase in the number of youth still engaged in a life of faith at the age of thirty.

In reality, there are not just two scenarios but hundreds of them. I chose two obviously contrasting scenarios to make it clear that many youth ministries don't trust the Holy Spirit for the genuine transformation of young people. Especially in

A lot of teenagers drop out of church because they view Christianity as a list of rules. They think it's just a boring anti-partying life. I don't think they really know that Christianity isn't a religion but that it's a relationship. Many teenagers feel like the church is more concerned about telling them what to do than being interested in who they are as a person.

EMILY, 13 YEARS OLD

North America we're too impatient to wait on the Holy Spirit, so we take things into our own hands.

We have the awesome responsibility of working with the youth entrusted to us, but ultimately the kids belong to the Lord. We're simply stewards. Be faithful when God assigns a young person to you, have faith when God chooses someone else, and ask God for wisdom to know the difference between the two. God is sovereign; God's work will be accomplished in the life of young people regardless of whether it's through us that God chooses to work. The Holy Spirit works to make something beautiful out of our feeble attempts to be faithful disciples and leads us to truth, unfolding the kingdom of God before us at a level we and our kids can understand. The Holy Spirit transforms us when we say yes to Jesus' invitation to come and follow him, and he breathes life into our missional purpose. Transformation in the life of adolescents is not possible, surely not sustainable without the inner working of the Holy Spirit.

A youth worker who serves as a spiritual guide actively seeks the involvement of the Holy Spirit in every aspect of ministry, surrendering to the Holy Spirit's work in transforming our youth. Transformational youth ministry isn't ultimately about our talents, programs, resources and experiences, but about young people encountering the presence of God and submitting to the work of the Holy Spirit in their lives.

While we can acknowledge this concept mentally, we usually find it more difficult to live out. Large numbers of North American evangelicals have seemingly written off the importance of the Holy Spirit's work among God's people.

NURTURING ENVIRONMENTS FOR SPIRITUAL TRANSFORMATION

For several years now the staff at YouthFront has intentionally focused on the necessity of trusting the Holy Spirit to transform young people. We have explored and experimented with developing environments that create opportunities for youth to experience the presence of God through body, soul and spirit. We share with them the idea of sacred space, a thin place where heaven and earth meet, where God's presence is so real that the place and encounter take on profound sacredness. It might be a natural space such as a mountain, a river, a prairie full of wild flowers.

> When the Spirit of truth comes, he will guide you into all the truth; for he will not speak on his own, but will speak whatever he hears, and he will declare to you the things that are to come. He will glorify me, because he will take what is mine and declare it to you.
>
> **JOHN 16:13-14**

It may be a labyrinth or prayer chapel. It might contain overt symbols of transcendence such as fire or incense. Sacred space can also be more subtle, leaving room for imagination and creative interplay with the Holy Spirit. One of the most exciting projects has been reshaping a 600-acre portion of one of our YouthFront camps into a place where youth can experience the presence of the divine. It's a place dedicated to seeking God face to face.

SACRED SPACES IN THE BIBLE

The idea of creating a sacred space occurs early and often in Scripture. In Genesis 12, God called Abram to leave his country and go to a land that God would show him. When Abram arrived in Canaan, the Lord appeared to him. Abram built an altar and worshiped the Lord. This location became a sacred space, a place where Abram met and communed with God.

> The Holy Spirit speaks to me through Scripture, words, whispers and creation. Learning that God speaks to us in so many ways has taught me to pay attention to what God wants to show me even through little things I didn't see before.
>
> **JOSH, COLLEGE STUDENT**

After this encounter with God, some time passed and Abram went to Egypt, where he got into some trouble. Abram left Egypt and returned to the sacred space where he had first encountered the Lord. He again called on the name of the Lord.

Abram, whose name was changed by God to Abraham, undoubtedly spoke to his children about experiencing the presence of God at Bethel. Later, Abraham's grandson Jacob was on a pilgrimage and had his own encounter with God. While Jacob was sleeping, he had a dream in which the Lord God appeared to him.

> Then Jacob woke from his sleep and said, "Surely the LORD is in this place—and I did not know it!" And he was afraid, and said, "How awesome is this place! This is none other than the house of God, and this is the gate of heaven." So Jacob rose early in the morning, and he took the stone that he had put under his head and set it up for a pillar and poured oil on the top of it. He called that place Bethel. (Gen 28:16-19)

Many years later Jacob found himself in a stressful situation with his father-in-law, Laban. God appeared to him again in a dream, saying, "I am the God of Bethel, where you anointed a pillar and made a vow to me. Now leave this land at once and return to the land of your birth" (Gen 31:13).

After Jacob resettled in the land of his birth, he found himself in challenging situations like his father did. When Jacob sought help from the Lord, God directed him to settle in Bethel and make an altar to the Lord there.

Jacob, sensing that he was coming again to this sacred space, purged all the idols from his family's belongings. Jacob prepared to meet God. When Jacob came into the presence of God he was told that his name would be changed from Jacob to Israel. God then made Israel a promise, "The land that I gave to Abraham and Isaac I will give to you, and I will give the land to your offspring after you" (Gen 35:15).

Jacob set up a stone pillar where the Lord had spoken to him. He poured a drink offering and oil on it, and Jacob called the place where God had spoken with him Bethel.

God often meets his people in such unique ways that the location of the encounter becomes a symbol of God's work in their lives just as they did for Abraham and Jacob.

DIVERSITY OF SACRED SPACES

When we're spiritual guides for youth, our guidance comes from the fullness of our own Christian experiences. As we seek to meet God face to face and dwell in his presence, we won't be wondering how to nurture sacred spaces. They'll flow from natural expressions of who we are and our individual passions for being with God.

I can look back over my three-plus-decade journey with Christ and name one place after another along the way where Christ met me in a significant way. There is a spot at a YouthFront camp where God spoke to me as a nineteen-year-old kid; that spot is just as meaningful to me today as it was thirty-some years ago. There is a sacred space near a cabin at the Lake of the Ozarks where I met with God often. Remembering that location brings back memories of great spiritual impact. I made twenty-one pilgrimages to the land of the Bible. All the memories of times spent in prayer at the Sea of Galilee, Jerusalem, and the empty tomb flow easily in my thoughts. I've had amazing experiences at the Mamertine Prison of Paul in Rome, Berchtesgaden in the Bavarian Alps, and the Conception Abbey north of Kansas City. All of these are sacred spaces for me because I encountered God there in unique ways.

Through the goodness of God, two years ago I found myself with

Not long ago I was in a worship environment that I really love—quiet and contemplative, an atmosphere that usually draws me into the presence of God. However, this time I was restless.

Frustrated, I cried out to God and just listened. I sensed that the Holy Spirit wanted me to go outside. I was confused, but I obeyed and sat down on a bench outside the chapel. I was silent; literally I couldn't speak, because I heard God saying, "I just want to be alone with you." All I could do was smile and look up at a sky full of stars.

God whispered the most beautiful things to me about my worth and who he thought I was. Since I was a little girl, I've longed for my dad to sit with me and be that affectionate. God revealed himself to me as my heavenly Father.

ASHLEY, COLLEGE STUDENT

several days in Ireland with no agenda other than to devote myself to researching and experiencing Celtic spirituality. The history of Christianity on the Emerald Island is rich, dating back to Saint Patrick in the fifth century, Saint Ciaran and Saint Kevin in the sixth century, and the early missionary movement that came out of Ireland to England, Scotland and ultimately the European continent.

One of my favorite places in Ireland is Glendalough, a contemplative community established by Saint Kevin in the sixth century. The reputation of Saint Kevin and his monastery attracted a growing number of pilgrims, ultimately making Glendalough into a great monastic city. He was abbot of Glendalough until his death at (according to legend) 120 years of age. His house and the cell where he prayed can still be seen. I spent two days drinking in the beauty and solitude of Glendalough. I clearly remember encountering the presence of God in the sacred spaces at Glendalough on numerous occasions.

Christian pilgrims have for centuries visited the seven churches located around this monastic city. Throughout the area, on the hillsides and around the lakes, are sacred spaces, places where worshipers spend time in prayer and solitude, encountering a holy God.

Being in Glendalough and the other places I have mentioned has deepened my desire to develop sacred spaces so that youth also may encounter the presence of God and be transformed. Our young people need youth workers who will diligently create environments that enable them to "be still and know that I am God" (Ps 46:10), sacred spaces where they might return year after year to commune with God.

SACRED SPACE AT THE ALTAR

One of the events we offer at YouthFront is the Altar. Let me walk you through one of my experiences there.

Torches lit the path as my wife and I made our way to evening worship at the lake. Young people began to line the shore and the dam. I could hear a guitar, then a violin—beautiful, peaceful. A solitary star appeared as the sun slipped below the horizon. A growing mist rose off the lake, creating a surreal image. The worship leader led us through an examination of three powerful metaphors for God: water, fire and wind.

> Midday is a time to gather with others in the presence of God. I love the quiet solitude. I always find this practice to be spiritual medicine to my soul.
>
> VALENTINE, COLLEGE STUDENT

Fire.

> The Lord went in front of them in a pillar of cloud by day, to lead them along the way, and in a pillar of fire by night, to give them light. (Ex 13:21)

After we read Hebrews 12:29, "For indeed our God is a consuming fire," a floating bonfire was ignited in the middle of the lake, wrapped in fog, shooting flames into the darkening sky. Amazing! We prayed a song asking God to breathe his peace on us followed by several minutes of silence for contemplation. Then a new song began, this time with bullfrogs, crickets and whippoorwills as the musicians. An owl hooted in the distance, bats flew overhead and fish periodically broke the surface of the water, all as if they had been waiting for their cue to participate in the worship of our great God.

Water.

Everyone who drinks of this water will be thirsty again, but those who drink of the water that I will give them will never be thirsty. The water that I will give will become in them a spring of water gushing up to eternal life. (Jn 4:13-14)

A number of us ambled to the water's edge or to water receptacles, immersing our hands or drinking to remind us that Jesus satisfies our thirst. Some washed their hands to symbolize their desire for clean hands and a pure heart. Others poured water over their heads, remembering their baptism into Christ.

Wind.

The wind blows where it chooses, and you hear the sound of it, but you do not know where it comes from or where it goes. So it is with everyone who is born of the Spirit. (Jn 3:8)

The Hebrew word for wind is the same word for breath. God breathed into Adam the breath of life. We reached out to feel the gentle breezes around us and then put our hands to our mouths to feel our own breath in the chilly evening. The God of the universe has breathed life into us. We felt God's nearness. We sensed God's presence.

All around, young people—some standing, some sitting, some on their knees, a few prostrate on the ground—encountered the presence of God.

Even though the fire floating on the lake was obviously ferocious, I couldn't feel any warmth. The Holy Spirit reminded me that even when we don't feel the warmth of God's presence, nor experience any physical manifestation of God's nearness, God is with us. God is forever ablaze, breathing life into us, at work in the world, ushering in the kingdom of God. Hallelujah!

CREATING SACRED SPACES

A sacred space doesn't have to be in a foreign country or in a massive cathedral or a breathtaking natural setting, however. Sacred spaces might not even be physical. A schedule that allows for quiet, rest (something that adolescents desperately need in our culture) and time to listen helps youth be attentive to their feelings, to their thoughts and especially to the still small voice of the Holy Spirit. Sacred space is an environment that nurtures attentiveness to the transcendent nature of God and draws us into the mystery of the Almighty. Aside from the location, we can create a sacred space through art, music, fragrance, fire, water, quiet and whatever other ways we may be inspired to try.

Creating a sacred space doesn't have to be—and probably shouldn't be—complex. In fact, according to the Old Testament, one of the most treasured of all sacred spaces was empty space. It was located above the Ark of the Covenant, kept in the inner most Holy of Holies in the temple, but it had no physical component to it. What had no physical expression was in reality the presence of the Almighty God.

We encouraged the young people at one retreat to meditate on a passage of Scripture while walking through the wooded trails. One young woman was irritated by this assignment but was willing to give it a try. Her passage of Scripture was John 13:1-20, which contains the account of Jesus washing his disciples feet. Later she shared her experience with the rest of us.

Not only was this young woman irritated by this assignment, she was irritated by her life. She admitted that she didn't love herself and had little faith that God could feel any differently about her than she did. Her deeper issue was thus yielding to the loving embrace of God and accepting that she could be loved by God.

After a while her commitment to keep her mind on the story of Jesus humbly washing the feet of his disciples began to soothe her anxious heart. The story eventually turned from Jesus washing the feet of his beloved disciples to Jesus desiring to wash her feet. She responded, "No, Jesus! I don't deserve to have you wash my feet. I don't deserve this kind of love from you. I've failed miserably as a disciple. You don't need to wash my feet. You can't. I'm not worthy."

She wept as she continued, describing how, at the precise moment she was refusing the love of Jesus through washing her feet, she looked down at her sandaled feet, wet with the morning dew. She sensed Jesus speaking directly to her: "My daughter, I have already washed your feet."

There weren't too many dry eyes when she finished telling the story of how God met her in the woods through her meditation and prayer.

There are many things you can do to create environments for young people to experience as sacred space. Use religious symbols—crosses (crucifixes or Latin, Celtic or Jerusalem style), Celtic designs, the ichthus, a crown of thorns, alpha and omega in Greek lettering, a chalice and bread—in your places of worship. Develop a prayer room filled with art and poetry, created by your youth if possible. Placing interactive things in these prayer rooms can be very powerful and transformational: add a paper shredder and encourage youth to write about personal struggles and then shred them as an act of confession and forgiveness.

If you don't have enough space for an enclosed prayer room, you can create smaller art installations or worship spots. In a corner of the room set up a place for a bowl of water. Place Scripture about baptism and cleansing around the water, along with instructions for youth to remember their baptism or symbolically wash their hands. Create a Wailing Wall, a place for youth to pray and attach their written prayers.

Use art, special lighting and music to create environments conducive to worship and prayer. Recently our church commissioned fourteen adult and fourteen young people to create art for the stations of the cross. Two works of art, one by an adult and one by a young person, were placed at each station to help facilitate meditation and contemplation. The stations of the cross were spread all over the church, and young and old were encouraged to walk through during Passion Week.

Sometimes simply using ambient music sets a subtle environment conducive to help people focus on God. Candles also help. Often we drape a room with cloth to add uniqueness to the environment. Tactile components, such as the laying-on of hands, shaping and molding clay, or oil for use in anointing participants, can significantly add to the symbolism of a worship

I have been in church my whole life. I remember praying the sinner's prayer and asking Jesus to come into my heart. But I really feel like I have been a symbolic Christian. . . . Today, I was praying, meditating and walking the stations of the cross. . . . I arrived at the station which focused on Christ stumbling under the weight of the cross. The verse I kept meditating on was Mark 8:34, "If any want to become my followers, let them deny themselves and take up their cross and follow me." . . . Then it hit me as if Jesus was speaking these words audibly, to me—"Erin, if you want to be my follower, deny yourself, pick up your cross and follow me." . . . I have never been willing to pick up my cross and deny myself. I said, "Yes Jesus, I want to be your follower."

ERIN, A HIGH SCHOOL JUNIOR

experience and may result in a transformation moment.

We must not think we can dim the lights, play recorded contemplative music, light a few candles and burn some incense and then assume we've created an environment that will magically transform our youth. These things will simply be the latest gimmicks unless you teach the symbolism and theology behind them.

For example, I love being in an environment that's lit only by candles, but it's important for me to speak to my youth about transcendence and mystery, to teach them about the metaphor of fire, to describe how the early church gathered in the dark catacombs to worship Christ. Something significant happens when young people associate their experience in a dimly lit environment with the experience of their Christian ancestors under persecution.

Fire. Every adolescent seems to be fascinated by fire. Why is that? Probably because fire is powerful, mysterious, mesmerizing, dangerous, transcendent and beautiful. Bonfires, candles and flames of any sort create environments conducive to contemplating the powerful, mysterious, mesmerizing, dangerous, transcendent and beautiful nature of God. A. W. Tozer acknowledges the potency of fire as a biblical symbol.

> God's holiness is so ineffable that no comparisons or figures will avail to express it. In fire He appeared at the burning bush; in the pillar of fire He dwelt through all the long wilderness journey. The fire that glowed between the wings of the cherubim in the holy place was called the Shekinah, the Presence, through the years of Israel's glory, and when the Old had given place to the New, He came at Pentecost as a fiery flame and rested upon each disciple.[1]

Share references in the Scriptures to fire—the burning bush, the pillar of fire, fire as judgment, the role of fire in sacrifices, fire as comfort and protection, tongues of fire at Pentecost, and descriptions of God using fire metaphors. The Bible contains more than five hundred verses about fire.

Incense. Incense is another element youth workers are incorporating into worship; however, when we fail to teach its significance, the beauty of its meaning is lost. Incense existed long before it was used in the 1960s to hide the smell of marijuana. It's mentioned more than a hundred times in Scripture as an important part of worshiping God.

In Exodus 30:1 we see the Israelites instructed to make an altar of acacia wood for offering incense. It was used in both the tabernacle and temple worship of Almighty God as an important aspect of the Holy of Holies. Incense was a part of the grain offering in Old Testament sacrifices.

Incense is a metaphor for the fragrance of prayer: "Let my prayer be counted as incense before you" (Ps 141:2). The prayers of the saints are described in Revelation 5:8 as incense: "The four living creatures and the twenty-four elders fell before the Lamb, each holding a harp and golden bowls full of incense, which are the prayers of the saints." The death of Christ is called "a fragrant offering and sacrifice to God" (Eph 5:2). When young people realize that the frankincense we burn in a worship service was one of the gifts that the wise men brought for the baby Jesus, it takes on a new significance and adds to the depth of their worship experience.

If you offer consistent opportunities for youth to have space and time to hear from God, you'll be amazed at the results. Give your youth some time in sacred space, offering just a few simple instructions about meditating on Scripture. (See chapter eight for more on this practice.) Afterward give them an opportunity to share how the Holy Spirit spoke to them through the Scripture. You'll be blessed.

SEVEN

Connecting Youth to the Story of God

In an increasingly postmodern environment, the concept of a metanarrative, an all-encompassing story, is viewed with major skepticism. Postmodernists say that humanity is so diverse that every nation, community or group has a story and therefore a metanarrative is not possible or even needed.

I agree that every family, group (youth group for example) church, community, country and even continent has a story, but these don't exclude a grand, overarching story. In fact, the beauty of the individual stories comes to full realization in the context of the metanarrative of the story of God at work in the world.

The Bible offers a view of the world that deals with the big questions: Who are we? Where are we? What is wrong? What is the solution? These questions are vitally important to our youth today. If they don't have answers to these questions, how can they ultimately make sense out of their individual stories?

Regardless of the postmodern guru who says there can be no metanarrative, I find that today's youth are drawn to God's metanarrative. Teaching this grand story is much more effective for Christian formation than using behavior modification techniques or a list of do's and don'ts.

The church did a poor job of storytelling in the twentieth century, so that we find ourselves depending on other outlets, such as movies, for an intense encounter with a compelling story. Christians should be storytellers who constantly weave their individual stories into the story of God and his people. While emphasizing the importance of the metanarrative, however, we can't discount the power of the individual and community stories we discover along the way. These stories impact the way people find their connection to the metanarrative. Through these connections our youth will learn to see the world in a new way, the kingdom-of-God way. We must tell stories. We must help our youth tell stories. We must celebrate our stories.

> A lot of times adults don't realize that kids can be really serious Christians. I think they underestimate our brains and how much we can understand.
>
> **ERIC, 15 YEARS OLD**

The most obvious practices that help us connect youth to the story of God are prayer and Scripture. But evangelicals have forgotten—or ignored—some other ways to experience and enact the story of God.

FAMILY HEIRLOOMS

When I was a kid, I loved visiting my grandparents' home where all my aunts, uncles and cousins would gather for food and fun. Usually, after a big meal, my uncles would gather to watch a sports event on TV or do some other manly activity. My aunts, after the kitchen was cleaned, would gather around the dining room table and tell stories.

I loved hearing their stories, so I always wanted to be with my aunts. They told certain stories over and over again. Looking back, I see how these stories took on a life of their own, growing more animated with time. Certain aunts were assigned portions of stories to ensure they were told properly. "No, you tell that story. You tell it better." There was an organization and hierarchy to the stories. Some stories were more important than others. Some were sad; most were happy. The stories had much to say about what kind of family we were and what we valued.

Looking back I realize how formative those stories were and continue to be. They encompassed and perpetuated our traditions and values. These traditions take on life and survive through the telling of stories.

It's no different with the story of God and God's people. Traditions are the family heirlooms of God's people, and they help us tell our story. Paul reminds us to "stand firm and hold fast to the traditions that you were taught by us, either by word of mouth or by our letter" (2 Thess 2:15). Sadly, evangelicals of the twentieth century have largely forgotten or ignored tradition. If we're going to help our youth embrace a living faith, we must expose them to family heirlooms and traditions that not only shape their individual identity but connect them to the big picture of God and his people—and not just some of God's people, but the whole, big family with thousands of years of history behind it.

TRADITION VERSUS TRADITIONALISM

Of course numerous Scriptures caution us to not lose the commandments of God in order to maintain our traditions. Jesus had one conflict after another with the religious leaders of his day over this issue. They, along with many church leaders today, were focusing on the wrong kind of tradition, or more accurately they were focused on traditionalism. This is exemplified in the following encounter between Jesus and the religious leadership of his day:

Now when the Pharisees and some of the scribes who had

come from Jerusalem gathered around him, they noticed that some of his disciples were eating with defiled hands, that is, without washing them. (For the Pharisees, and all the Jews, do not eat unless they thoroughly wash their hands, thus observing the tradition of the elders; and they do not eat anything from the market unless they wash it; and there are also many other traditions that they observe, the washing of cups, pots, and bronze kettles.) So the Pharisees and the scribes asked him, "Why do your disciples not live according to the tradition of the elders, but eat with defiled hands?" He said to them, "Isaiah prophesied rightly about you hypocrites, as it is written,

> 'This people honors me with their lips,
> but their hearts are far from me;
> in vain do they worship me,
> teaching human precepts as doctrines.'

> You abandon the commandment of God and hold to human tradition."

Then he said to them, "You have a fine way of rejecting the commandment of God in order to keep your tradition!" (Mk 7:1-9)

We've all probably been in situations where we've wanted to go after the church leadership for making life miserable by holding onto some form of traditionalism. "We don't do that at our church," someone states, as if our entire faith will be lost if we move the youth group meeting to a different night or change the translation of the Bible we use.

Creating a presence-centered youth ministry will require us to discern between tradition and traditionalism. In his classic *Orthodoxy*, G. K. Chesterton writes:

> Tradition may be defined as an extension of the franchise. Tradition means giving votes to the most obscure of all classes, our ancestors. It is the democracy of the dead. Tradition refuses to submit to the small and arrogant oligarchy of those who merely happen to be walking about.[1]

In *Deconstructing Evangelicalism,* D. G. Hart examines the thoughts of a variety of evangelical scholars who call us to reconnect with tradition, including Thomas Howard:

> Lest he upset born-again readers, Howard made clear that in claiming evangelicalism to be insufficient he was not saying that born-again Protestantism was wrong. The movement's articles of faith, its piety and zeal were all commendable. But Christianity offered so much more than the bare essentials of doctrine, a strict reliance on the Bible as opposed to the wisdom of the ages, or evangelicalism's strict morality. There were, for instance, phenomena such as liturgical worship, prayer books, religious images, the sacraments, and the church calendar that, according to Howard, could supplement and deepen the simple piety of born-again Christians.[2]

> Tradition is the living faith of the dead, whereas traditionalism is the dead faith of the living.
>
> **JAROSLAV PELIKAN,**
> **YALE PROFESSOR OF**
> **HISTORY EMERITUS**

RECOVERING THE ROLE OF TRADITION

We can help connect youth to the story of God by recovering the role of tradition. Exposing our youth to the historic creeds, the beauty of liturgy, the power and meaning of the sacraments, and the time-tested discipline of spiritual practices will significantly impact their Christian formation. Let's consider them one by one.

Creeds. The Apostles' Creed filled a significant role in my Christian formation. Reciting it made me aware that what I believed was profound, beyond the bounds of this world, wonderful and, well, different. Its uniqueness intrigued me, formed me.

The Apostles' Creed provided stability for me. When I left the mainline church I had attended for many years to attend a conservative evangelical church, I was told the Apostles' Creed was Catholic and in conflict with the only thing we really need, the Bible. I heard stories about how the Reformation saved us from all sorts of nonsense like this. Years later, after studying Christian history and thought, I realized that the Reformers heartily embraced the Nicene and Apostles' Creed as vital for Christian profession.

Reformed theologian Michael Horton says that the Creed "deserves renewed attention," for it provides "a way of instructing a new generation in the essentials."

> On the eve of the Reformation, parents could not teach their children the creed because they themselves did not know it. The same is largely true in our day, as Gallup and similar pollsters have made painfully clear.[3]

The word *creed* originates from the Latin word *credo* which means "I believe." The Nicene and Apostles' creeds, birthed by the early church, are the best known. Creeds help connect our youth to the story of God; as we recite the creeds we identify with our brothers and sisters in Christ all over the world, not only in the present but also in the past and the future.

I in no way intend to place more value in the creeds than Scripture. Instead, the creeds *point to* the issues that I am willing to die for. Reciting creeds help our youth understand crucial doctrine. They condense truly important issues in a way that emphasizes the web of core Christian beliefs. More than that, creeds tether us to the story of God. When youth begin to stray, step out of the church, explore other religions, or consider putting aside Christianity, the Apostles' Creed pulls them back into awareness of the story of God.

Liturgy. *Liturgy* literally means "the work (service) of the people," relating to the organization of our worship and devotion to God. The beauty and tradition of liturgy appeals to many young people, but *liturgy* is another word that makes many evangelicals nervous. In the broadest sense it refers to prepared prewritten worship services, so any church that has a particular order of service has a liturgy, even if they claim they aren't a liturgical church.[4]

> I like that midday prayer gives me a chance to quietly reflect on things and just sit with God. I like hearing everyone declaring their faith in Christ together. I like reciting the Lord's Prayer and the Apostles' Creed, because now that I follow Christ, they mean much more to me.
>
> **TATE, COLLEGE STUDENT**

The book of Psalms, the prayer book for Jewish believers including Jesus himself, is the most important liturgical source we have. Several liturgical hymns are included in Scripture including Mary's hymn of praise known as the Magnificat (Lk 1:46-55) and Paul's hymn of Christ's humiliation and exaltation (Phil 2:5-11). The tradition of liturgy continued with the early church. The *Didache*, a treatise of apostolic teaching, was written early in the life of the new church and was in a sense the first book containing liturgy for the church.

Ray, a youth worker I am good friends with, was skeptical about using liturgy with his youth group until he read this quotation by one of his favorite Christian authors, A. W. Tozer:

I have observed that our familiar impromptu service, planned by the leader twenty minutes before, often tends to follow a ragged and tired order almost as standardized as the Mass. The liturgical service is at least beautiful; ours is often ugly. [The liturgical service] has been carefully worked out through the centuries to capture as much of beauty as possible and to preserve a spirit of reverence among the worshipers. In the majority of our meetings there is scarcely a trace of reverent thought, no recognition of the unity of the body, little sense of the divine presence, no moment of stillness, no solemnity, no wonder, no holy fear.[5]

Ray now uses traditional liturgy on a regular basis in his youth ministry practice to connect youth to the story of God.

The concern for some is that liturgy becomes dry ritual, but this isn't a problem solely with liturgy. Anything can become a lifeless ritual if it falls into the rut of activity without authenticity. On the flip side, churches that seek to eliminate tradition, creeds, symbols, liturgy and other wonderful family heirlooms of our faith offer a shallow example of Christianity and lose a wonderful opportunity to connect to the story of God. I have many friends who have left traditionless, nonliturgical, symbol-void churches for churches that value the richness of Christian tradition and aesthetically appealing environments.

In addition to exposing your youth to ancient liturgies of our faith, we should encourage young people to create new liturgy for their communities. Creating liturgy can be as simple as having the youth write prayers or submit poetry to use for certain purposes or at specific times. We might be surprised at the beauty that surfaces from our youth and becomes a part of the group identity. We can recruit creative people in the congregation to nurture our youth and harness their creativity for community worship. Allowing youth to participate helps them feel linked to their faith community and ultimately to the story of God.

Sacraments. Sacraments are Christian practices attached to the promise of grace. The Catholic and Orthodox churches embrace seven sacraments: baptism, the Eucharist, confirmation, confession, anointing the sick, marriage and holy orders. Protestants generally hold to baptism and the Eucharist as the only Christ-instituted sacraments.

One big question is how God works through sacraments. When we consider the modern mindset, which places high value on the quest to know and rationally explain things that in actuality are quite transcendent, it's no wonder Christians disagree concerning the exact nature, number and meaning of sacraments.

Today's young people suffer little consternation about our inability to fully understand the mechanics of sacraments. Unhindered by rationalism that discounts metaphysical reality, young people easily celebrate and revel in the beauty, depth and awe of the Eucharist worship. Baptism properly explained to our youth becomes a major life event of intense significance.

Protestants have been so hesitant to attach spiritual implications to anything connected with physical matter and experience that we have played down the significance and depth of the sacraments' impact on our lives. God is at work to restore and renew all things, which will result in us moving from a reality that holds to a few sacraments to a reality that views and holds all things as sacramental.

We have misdirected energy toward defining ourselves based on what we do or don't do instead of defining ourselves by who we belong to and who we are in Christ. We should help our youth embrace a holistic spirituality, a way of life that seeks to do everything for the glory of God (1 Cor 10:31). Teaching our youth to examine their spirituality based on cooperating with God in the renewal of all things is much healthier than defining a spiritual life based on not drinking or not smoking or not watching MTV. As we work with young people, we've been guilty of pathetic cultural pettiness rather than helping young people see how they fit into the drama of the ages. We're called to cooperate with the One who holds all things together, to work alongside the firstborn of all creation to reconcile all things to himself.

God dwells among us and is in the process of restoring all things, things we'll inherit as his children. We're moving from a life with a few sacraments to a life that is sacramental. Let's guide youth in that direction by helping them view all aspects of life as sacred.

SPIRITUAL PRACTICES

A more familiar (and for evangelicals, more comfortable) way of connecting students to the story of God involves spiritual disciplines and practices. This should not, however, be viewed as an individual quest to become more spiritual. Young people need to see themselves as part of a unique community of followers of Jesus, which involves seeking the presence of God and embracing as a community the values of the kingdom of God. Eddie Gibbs writes,

> We may admire from afar the dedication of monks and nuns to their daily routine, with time allocated throughout the day and night for times of prayer. We may even benefit from visiting a house of prayer for a retreat lasting a few days. But how can their disciplines be made accessible to people who earn their living and meet their pressing family responsibilities in the

workaday world? As a starting point, the insight of Diogenes Allen is pertinent. He says the main purpose of the contemplative life is "to perceive all things in relation to God and to know God's continuous presence through them." It is this integration that is sadly lacking within contemporary Western Christianity. Many laypersons find that the church is disconnected from the issues that concern them through the remainder of the week.[6]

Christian practices aren't exclusively for a community setting, but when we engage in Christian practices individually we are still part of a community of people who are doing life with God together. We don't engage in Christian practices to get God to love us more and show us favor. God's love for us and our youth is perfect. Christian practices are a way to celebrate and worship God while conforming to the image of God. We engage in Christian practices because Jesus calls us to them. Christian practices move us into alignment with God's intentions for us and help us to realize what it means to become fully human. Christian practices necessitate all of who we are—body, soul, emotions, spirit, intellect, heart and experience.

> Do you not know that in a race the runners all compete, but only one receives the prize? Run in such a way that you may win it. *Athletes exercise self-control* in all things; they do it to receive a perishable wreath, but we an imperishable one. So I do not run aimlessly, nor do I box as though beating the air; but I punish my body and enslave it, so that after proclaiming to others I myself should not be disqualified. (1 Corinthians 9:24-27, emphasis added)

I have always been an athlete. I was dedicated to the sports I played; practice for basketball, baseball and football all consumed many hours of my time. But then I broke my leg the summer before my freshman year of high school, and football was ruled out for at least a year. Knowing I would go crazy not playing a sport, I asked the doctor if there were any sports I could participate in. He suggested swimming because it would be good for my rehabilitation.

I remember the first day of high school swimming practice. I thought swimming would be fun—playing tag, jumping off the diving board. The coach announced that he intended to see some of us die on this first day. I kind of chuckled as he proceeded to tie up our feet so that we would begin our swim with only our hands. It wasn't long before we were all sick.

He announced that we could untie our legs. *Thank God that's over,* I thought. Coach then sadistically announced that the assistants would now tie our arms behind our backs so we only had the use of our legs. I will never forget the first time I threw up in a pool, and I wasn't the only one. There is nothing fun about swimming with your hands tied behind your back, trying to gulp for air and avoid the chunks of vomit floating on the surface. Welcome to your first day of swimming practice.

> We too easily get comfortable in our faith, after all Jesus has already saved us. We forget that we are instructed in Philippians 2:12 to take seriously the responsibility to continue to work out our salvation.
>
> **CHRIS, COLLEGE STUDENT**

I wanted to quit but I didn't. I would eventually stand out in swimming, becoming the captain of my high school team, setting school records and gaining notoriety in the media. In fact, I dropped out of all other high school sports to pursue swimming full time (chicks dig guys in Speedos). I was in the pool everyday, practicing and paying the price to excel. Through the practices of my life I became enculturated into the life of a competitive swimmer.

In Henri Nouwen's book *Compassion: A Reflection on the Christian*

Life, he discusses disciplines as the means by which we are habituated into a compassionate way of life.

> In the Christian life, discipline is the human effort to unveil what has been covered, to bring to the foreground what has remained hidden, and to put on the lampstand what has been kept under a basket. It is like raking away the leaves that cover the pathways in the garden of our soul. Discipline enables the revelation of God's divine Spirit in us. Discipline in the Christian life does indeed require effort, but it is an effort to reveal rather than to conquer. God always calls. To hear his call and allow that call to guide our actions requires discipline in order to prevent ourselves from remaining or becoming spiritually deaf. There are so many voices calling for our attention and so many activities distracting us that a serious effort is necessary if we are to become and remain sensitive to the divine presence in our lives.[7]

When young people incorporate spiritual practices into their lives they work to habituate a way of life in Jesus. The practices of faith nurture a passion and love for Jesus Christ and an awareness of God's divine presence. The practices of faith are very much a part of working out our salvation.

> Therefore, my beloved, just as you have always obeyed me, not only in my presence, but much more now in my absence, work out your own salvation with fear and trembling; for it is God who is at work in you, enabling you both to will and to work for his good pleasure. Do all things without murmuring and arguing, so that you may be blameless and innocent, children of God without blemish in the midst of a crooked and perverse generation, in which you shine like stars in the world. (Phil 2:12-15)

What are the practices that youth workers as spiritual guides should expose youth to, and how do we do this in such a way that our students will incorporate them into their lives? How do we get kids to embrace Christian practices, some of which may be 2,000 years old, without freaking them out?

I have taken hundreds of young people on pilgrimages to the Middle East. One of the favorite experiences they have is going to the Valley of Elah to search for smooth stones out of the brook that still runs through the valley. We then read the account in 1 Samuel 17 of young David fighting Goliath.

David had the faith to take on Goliath to honor the name of the Lord. Those around David wanted to help him prepare for the fight by equipping him with Saul's armor. One problem: David staggered under the weight of the oversized armor. This equipment didn't work for David. What worked for David was a slingshot, a bag and five smooth stones.

David had confidence facing Goliath with the tools that he had become very familiar with. His slingshot and stones equipped him to serve faithfully in what he had been called to do. In the remainder of the book we will examine many Christian practices and disciplines. Serving as an effective spiritual guide for youth does not require that you perfect all of the spiritual practices. You need things that work for you, and so do your youth. We need discernment to not force ineffective armor on ourselves or the youth who look to us for leadership. At the same time, it's good to develop a rhythm of exposing ourselves along with our youth to new spiritual practices. You never know when you'll stumble on just the right disciplines for you or your youth.

EIGHT

Prayer Practices for Presence-Centered Youth Ministry

The National Study of Youth and Religion revealed that 80 percent of all American teenagers pray. According to studies by the American Bible Society, 91 percent of American teenagers who pray believe that their prayers are answered. When asked how they pray, a majority of teenagers speak of making up personal prayers. The most common things they pray for are sick loved ones and personal needs.

The good news is that so many young people consider prayer a legitimately important aspect of their lives. The bad news is that so many of these young people are not being taught what prayer is, nor are they being shown how to pray. Adolescence is a critical time to help young people develop a meaningful and genuine prayer life.

It seems like an overwhelming challenge to teach youth to pray without ceasing when so many Christians view prayer as a personal list of things we want God to do for us. We systematically go through our lists making requests much like a child seated on the lap of Santa Claus in a shopping mall. Prayer is so much more than this. Christianity has developed rich and meaningful prayer practices and exercises over the last two thousand years. Let's examine some ways to approach God in prayer.

LISTENING TO GOD THROUGH SILENCE AND SOLITUDE

Young people are extremely busy living in today's world. Their schedules are complex and intense in a way that used to be an issue only for the busiest adults trying to get ahead in the world. On top of family and academic schedules, youth are piling on music, sports, social events, jobs and church activities. Kids are under stress that was unknown to previous adolescent generations.

No doubt young people living in agrarian cultures of the past worked hard and long hours. However, the nature of their lifestyles allowed for mental space and quiet time to think. Today's teenagers are inundated by nearly constant noise

> I like that midday marks the middle of my day, in the midst of the chaos of my life. I am drawn to the peaceful atmosphere of prayer and meditation.
>
> **LYNELLE, COLLEGE STUDENT**

and stress, not conducive to mental or spiritual space. Young people, like everyone else, need silence and solitude to be able to hear God and to be attentive to God's presence.

The power of solitude and silence is apparent in one of Elijah's experiences. The Lord did not meet Elijah in the strong wind, the powerful earthquake or the consuming fire. God came to Elijah through sheer silence.

> Now there was a great wind, so strong that it was splitting mountains and breaking rocks in pieces before the LORD, but the LORD was not in the wind; and after the wind an earthquake, but the LORD was not in the earthquake; and after the earthquake a fire, but the LORD was not in the fire; and after the

fire a sound of sheer silence. When Elijah heard it, he wrapped his face in his mantle and went out and stood at the entrance of the cave. (1 Kings 19:11-13)

A significant part of solitude is listening. In the 1980s Dan Rather interviewed Mother Teresa. Rather asked her, "What do you say to God when you pray?"

Mother Teresa responded, "I don't say anything. I listen."

Rather followed up with another question, "Then, what does Jesus say to you?"

After a short pause, Mother Teresa said, "He doesn't say anything either. He just listens." Later she said, "Before you speak, it is necessary for you to listen, for God speaks in the silence of the heart."

There is something so powerful about what Mother Teresa said. A relationship with Jesus is first and foremost about abiding in his presence. Communication through silence or whispering can happen only through intimacy and proximity. My wife and I have been married for thirty years. Some of our most powerful communication comes as a result of our deep level of love and intimacy when we know what each other is thinking and neither one of us has to utter a word. We can't hear God's still small voice from a distance.

> I like the fact that everyone gathers together for midday prayer. Community is very important to me. I like the stillness and peacefulness at this time of the day.
>
> **AMANDA, COLLEGE STUDENT**

Soon after the opening verses in his Gospel, Mark describes the intense activity as Jesus ministered in Galilee with his disciples in tow. Jesus was teaching, healing people, casting out demons, dealing with his disciples' family members, traveling and preaching, constantly surrounded by those in need. A busy day ends with the whole city gathered at the door of Peter's house where Jesus continued to heal the sick and cast out demons.

And then we come to this verse: "In the morning, while it was still very dark, he got up and went out to a deserted place, and there he prayed." This is the rhythm of Jesus' spirituality. Jesus sought solitude, time alone with his Father.

When his disciples found him, we learn that his time of intimacy with the Father empowered him to continue his mission. "He answered, 'Let us go on to the neighboring towns, so that I may proclaim the message there also; for that is what I came out to do.' And he went throughout Galilee, proclaiming the message in their synagogues and casting out demons" (Mk 1:38-39). If Jesus needed solitude; we need it too.

This might seem overly simplistic, but if I had to select only one practice to implement in our youth ministries, I'd pick listening prayer in silence and solitude. Start with two minutes of silence during a gathering, and gradually increase the time as your youth become familiar with the practice. When we create an environment where we and our youth make silence and solitude a significant part of prayer practice, we'll discover the transformational nature of this discipline.

> The careful balance between silence and words, withdrawal and involvement, distance and closeness, solitude and community forms the basis of the Christian life and should therefore be the subject of our most personal attention.
>
> **HENRI J. M. NOUWEN,** *OUT OF SOLITUDE*

IMAGINATIVE PRAYER

Ignatius of Loyola is a fascinating character. He was born in 1491 in the castle of Loyola, the youngest of thirteen kids. At sixteen he went to serve the treasurer of Castile, a kingdom ruled by King Ferdinand. Ignatius's privileges as nobility led to a passion for fine food, fine women, gambling and mischievousness. His aspiration was to become a great military leader.

In the same year that Martin Luther was writing his Ninety-Five Theses, Ignatius joined the army to pursue his dream of becoming a military hero. In 1521, while defending the citadel in Pamplona a cannonball ripped between Ignatius' lower legs. He chose the long-suffering road of surgery and rehabilitation over amputation, so he could continue pursuing his dreams of military greatness. During his lengthy convalescence, Ignatius read tales of knights accomplishing heroic military feats. He used his imagination to place himself in the stories.

At some point during his recovery, he read *Life of Christ* by Ludolf of Saxony. Ignatius used his imagination, as he had done previously, to enter the stories of the Gospels and the lives of famous saints. He began to realize that his imaginations with the Gospel stories led to a different result from his imaginations of military exploits. The stories of Jesus and the early saints produced feelings of joy, love and peace. After seeing a vision of Mary with the baby Jesus in her arms, Ignatius experienced transformation and conversion.

As soon as Ignatius of Loyola was able, he went to Montserrat to write down, confess and repent of all of his sins, which took him three days. When he had finished, Ignatius stripped off his clothes of a nobleman and put on the clothes of a peasant. He laid his sword and knife on the altar and renounced his former life.

He then spent a year in the caves around Manresa using Ludolf of Saxony's writings to develop practices of prayer that would enable him to encounter God and grow spiritually. This was the beginning of his influential *Spiritual Exercises*.

Ignatius became very focused on being present with God. He nurtured his awareness of God at work in his life and the world around him. At the end of his year in Manresa, he felt compelled to make a pilgrimage to Jerusalem. He walked from Spain to Jerusalem in order to pray and to use the *Spiritual Exercises* in the land of the Bible.

Ignatius was not an educated man theologically and was not needed in Jerusalem. He was there less than two weeks when he was ordered to leave by a church authority. Crushed, Ignatius determined that he would get the theological training he needed so he would never be expelled again. He then proceeded to get kicked out of one theological school after another because he wouldn't tow the party line.

Before long, however, students flocked to him and were grateful for the impact of *Spiritual Exercises* on their spiritual devotion. He eventually took a vow of poverty in 1534 with a small group of brothers. In 1540, the pope recognized the group as the Society of Jesus. The order grew dramatically after his death.

Ignatius's *Spiritual Practices* feature his practice of imaginative prayer, which involves yielding all of ourselves—including our creativity—to the Holy Spirit and Scripture. A part of the desire to be fully human is to use all of our divinely given senses to encounter God. Jesus often told stories to energize the creativity in people, to make them think differently and to engage their imagination. Imaginative prayer is easy to learn, and adolescents are responsive to it, so it's an especially effective spiritual practice for this age group.

When I practice imaginative prayer, I often select a Scripture passage that I want to spend time meditating on and praying through. I prefer to focus on the Gospels for imaginative prayer, particularly parables such as the good Samaritan and the prodigal son, or narratives involving the birth, life, ministry, death and resurrection of Jesus. To begin, I first make myself totally available—body, mind, soul and spirit—to the Holy Spirit. Then I imagine what it must have been like to live in the situation described in the passage. I interact with the text of Scripture, contemplating it, asking questions like these:

- What do I see?

- What do I smell?

- What sounds do I hear?

- What is the weather like?

- What are the landscape and surroundings like?

- Who do I see myself as in the passage? A specific, central character? A bystander?

- What am I doing?

- How am I reacting to the events?

- How do I feel about what is happening?

- What would I say to the Lord if he were standing nearby?

- What is the Lord saying to me?

I read the text several times as I ask these questions, being patient and taking time to listen. The focus of imaginative prayer is to be wholly engaged, present with your entire being. Imaginative prayer takes more than a few minutes. It takes some time to engage mentally and creatively, sometimes lots of time, but it can be powerfully transforming. (See the afterword for one such experience of imaginative prayer that changed my life and ministry.)

God has the power to work within us and "accomplish abundantly far more than all we can ask or imagine" (Eph 3:20-21). Is it possible for us to imagine God being greater than he actually is? Of course not; we're too limited. It is possible, though, that our imaginations could get us into trouble and idolatry. At the same time, our desire to know Christ and to comprehend him in a way that surpasses knowledge is not something we should give up to fear. Through imaginative prayer we can move our meditations out of the watered down realm of safety and into the realm where God is able to accomplish abundantly far more that all we can ask or imagine.

EXAMINATION OF CONSCIENCE

Saint Ignatius encouraged another prayer practice, called examination of conscience, for discerning the working of the Holy Spirit through both consolation and desolation.

> We recognize that there is properly spiritual consolation when the soul takes fire in the love of its Creator by some inner motion and then cannot love any creature but because of Him. Also when tears are shed, provoking that love, either because they come from sorrow with regard to sins, or from the meditation of Christ's Passion, or from whatever other cause that is rightly disposed for the worship and honor of God. Finally, any increase of faith, hope, and charity can also be called consolation; equally all joyfulness, which usually incites the soul to meditation on heavenly things, to zeal for salvation, to be at rest and peace with God.[1]

The examination of conscience is designed to help us discern the positive and passionate things of God and the working of the Holy Spirit that's taking place within us. We contemplate the times when we feel closest to God, when we feel fully alive in Christ. Many of us have used this practice before without knowing its origin, perhaps when we've asked our youth to share a highlight from a retreat. In this practice we notice when we're consumed with passion for Christ. We begin to detect patterns about what brings us closer to the love of Christ. We discern how we best connect to the ministry of the Holy Spirit within us. We're also reminded to maintain a spirit of humility in the midst of the joy of consolation.

Ignatius has these thoughts on spiritual desolation:

> Any obscuring of the soul, any disturbance, any instigation to inferioror earthly things, must be called spiritual desolation; likewise, any disquietude and agitation, or temptation leading to mistrust of salvation and to the expelling of hope and charity; and thus the soul feels itself becoming sad, tepid and apathetic, and almost despairing of the clemency of God Himself, its Creator. In fact, as desolation is opposed to consolation, so, also, all thoughts proceeding from each of them are directly opposed to one another.[2]

In this spiritual exercise we pray, listen and discern for those times when we seem to be furthest away from the love of God, when we're filled with worry and faithlessness, when we feel apathetic and without hope, when we feel desolation. Saint Ignatius offers three reasons feelings of desolation may occur:

- Desolation may be the result of being lazy and negligent in maintaining spiritual disciplines.

- It may be that we are being tested. The testing of our faith works patience.

- Desolation can serve as a reminder that consolation is not achieved through a formula. It's a gift from God, a gift of grace.[3]

Ignatius warns us not to make major decisions when we feel far from the Holy Spirit. During these times we should turn more intensely to prayer and meditation. These are the times to patiently trust God in faith.

So the examination of conscience is a prayer practice of discernment. The word *discern* comes from a Latin word that describes the process of detecting and sorting out information through the senses. We can teach spiritual examination to our youth and practice it with them. It's extremely effective in a group setting. I use this prayer exercise on mission trips and during camp experiences to lead adolescents into meditation and discernment of how the Holy Spirit is at work in their lives. I also use it in casual conversations with groups of young people to move a conversation toward spiritual issues. I ask questions like these:

- What are some things you've done this week that made you feel fully alive?
- What has been the highlight of your week?
- Have you experienced anything lately that has robbed you of joy?
- What has been the most discouraging thing that has happened to you this week?

As conversations continue, I make pastoral connections that help young people discern God at work in their lives. This prayer exercise is also helpful to youth for discerning what their future vocation might be, a big issue for late adolescents.

RESPIRATORY PRAYER

In the centuries after Jesus' resurrection, his followers sought ways to commune deeply with God. One form of prayer, respiratory prayer, developed out of a desire to live out Paul's instruction in 1 Thessalonians 5:17: "Pray without ceasing." To be obedient to this command, his disciples prayed prayers that flowed as rhythmically as breathing. To these early Christians, who followed Christ at the constant risk of martyrdom, prayer *was* as important as breathing.

The most ancient prayer of this type is called the Jesus Prayer: "Lord Jesus Christ, Son of the Living God, have mercy on me, a sinner." There are several variations of the Jesus Prayer:

- Christ have mercy.

- Jesus, have mercy on me.

- Lord Jesus Christ, Son of God, have mercy on me, a sinner.

It's become my favorite prayer because of its simplicity and profoundness. This prayer has also been called the Prayer of the Heart because of the connection it has to the reality and rhythm of life. This prayer originates in the Gospels. Jesus encounters several people who use some variation of the phrase: the Canaanite woman (Mt 15:21-28), two blind men (Mt 20:29-34), ten lepers (Lk 17:11-19), the blind beggar outside of Jericho (Lk 18:35-43), and Bartimaeus (Mk 10:45-47). It's also found in the parable of the Pharisee and tax collector in the temple (Lk 18:9-14).

The more I pray this prayer the more I am reminded of the wonderful grace of God and my own weakness. I need mercy from the Lord Jesus Christ, Son of the living God. This prayer forms a never-ending loop of repentance and acknowledgment of the wonderful mercy of the Lord.

Respiratory prayers are usually said in association with the breathing rhythm. With the inhale, pray the first part, "Lord Jesus Christ, Son of the living God." With the exhale, pray the second part, "Have mercy on me, a sinner."

Jim, a youth pastor who works closely with YouthFront, shared this experience of the benefit from respiratory prayer. A teenager in his youth group was hospitalized with severe depression. Jim visited the young man in the hospital and witnessed his sense of total despair. He said, "Jim, I've tried to pray, but I can't."

Jim taught this young man the Jesus Prayer. Two days later, Jim got a call from the young man's parents who shared their son's progress.

It didn't solve all this young man's problems, but the prayer had an amazing impact on his condition.

Respiratory prayer can become an integral part of spirituality, for us and for the young people we work with. I often take portions of Scripture that have impacted me or phrases from meaningful songs or books and use them as respiratory prayers. Some of the respiratory prayers that I have prayed include

- The LORD is my shepherd, I shall not want (Ps 23:1).

- Lord, may my love be genuine, help me hate what is evil and hold fast to what is good (Rom 12:9).

- Let every word I speak to every person I meet be filled with kindness.

PRAYER ROPE

I have always been a touch-taste-feel kind of guy. My fingers keep busy. If they aren't tapping away on the computer keyboard, they may be drumming a beat, holding a book or picking at my finger-nails. In my younger days, I carried a smooth stone in my pocket to fiddle with. Several years ago, when I expanded my repertoire of prayer practices, I discovered the prayer rope, sometimes called a chotki, which complements my need to keep my hands moving.

The chotki, a necklace-like loop often made of wool, consists of fifty to a hundred complicated knots. Each individual knot is created by tying a series of nine small cross-knots. The purpose of the knots in the Eastern Orthodox tradition is to count the number of times the Jesus Prayer is prayed. On most chotkis there is a larger cross, made out of tight knots, and wooden beads marking specific numerical in-tervals between the knots. They can be found in other materials and designs, however.[4]

The creation of the first prayer rope for Christianity is usually attributed to Pachomius, a monk from Egypt in the fourth century. Pachomius was serving in the military when he was influenced by the love and good works of Christians in Thebes. As a result Pachomius promised God he would live his life the same way.

Eventually Pachomius sensed God wanted him to establish a monastic community. By the time he died of the plague, he had established eleven monasteries. Within a generation of his death, there were several thousand monasteries in and around Egypt. The monastic movement quickly spread throughout North Africa, the Middle East and into Europe. He is recognized today as a founder of Christian monasticism.

Saint Pachomius diligently nurtured a presence-centered environment that created opportunities for those in his community to encounter God and be transformed. Saint Pachomius is said to have created a prayer rope to enable his brothers and sisters to remember to follow Paul's instruction to pray without ceasing (1 Thess 5:17).

I have used the chotki prayer rope to create a wonderful practice that has become a significant part of my prayer life.

- I start with a knotted cross at the bottom of the loop, praying, "In the name of the Father and of the Son and of the Holy Spirit. Amen."
- At the top of the knotted cross is a wooden bead that reminds me to declare the Apostles' Creed.
- Between the first wooden bead and the second wooden bead are twenty-five knots. I recite the Jesus Prayer once for each knot.
- The second wooden bead reminds me to pray the Lord's Prayer.
- There are twenty-five more knots, then, that signal me to pray the Jesus Prayer.

- I have chosen to use the third wooden bead as a reminder to pray Psalm 23.

- The third wooden bead is followed by twenty-five more knots and twenty-five more recitations of the Jesus Prayer.

- I then come to the fourth wooden bead, which reminds me to pray the *Glory Be:* "Glory be to the Father and to the Son and to the Holy Spirit. As it was in the beginning, is now and shall be forever, world without end. Amen."

- Another twenty-five Jesus Prayer knots and I'm back at the first bead.

At this point I'm a third of the way through. On the next revolution, I pray the Jesus Prayer for each set of twenty-five knots as I did the first time around. When I come to the wooden beads I pray for my family: first for my wife, Vicki; then for our oldest son, Micah, and his wife Anne; then for our son Daniel and his wife Lindsay; and finally for our daughter, Jessica. On the final revolution the wooden beads remind me to pray for my spiritual walk with Christ, for friends and other family, for my ministry, and for needs around the world.

You might be thinking, *That sounds like a lot of prayer. It seems like it could easily just be a ritual that you hurry through.* For me, however, it has become a natural practice to keep me focused. My commute is my favorite time to pull out my prayer rope. When I'm kept waiting, I can pull it out of my pocket and begin praying. When I put my hand in my pocket, it reminds me to be in an attitude of prayer.

I'm not going into the detail about my chotki so you can teach this to your youth group next week. In fact, please don't. You'll probably just create problems for yourself. Can't you hear the rumors? "Pastor Tom is teaching our kids the rosary." (This isn't the rosary, by the way.) I share this because a chotki could potentially be one of your five smooth stones, one of the practices that equip you spiritually.

I've shared the practice of using a prayer rope with many older adolescents when I was significantly involved in their Christian formation. It usually surfaces as we're going about some ordinary task together. When one of them sees my chotki and asks what it's for, I tell them about it.

PRAYER POSTURES

Prayer should involve more than our minds and occasionally our tongues. In fact, having our bodies involved in prayer is essential. We communicate to God through our body language even if we aren't aware of what our bodies are saying. Being aware of our body language prepares us for prayer and adds a new dimension to our experience.

There is no doubt that our bodies play an important role when we approach the presence of God through prayer and worship. Christians have used their bodies to express devotion to God through the centuries.

> During a recent worship service we had a foot-washing service. There was no doubt in my mind that we were in the presence of God and that he was changing hearts during that service.
>
> KRISTEN, 18 YEARS OLD

Kneeling. Praying on bended knees expresses humble respect and reverence toward God. It's one of the most common postures mentioned in Scripture. Daniel (Dan 6:10), Solomon (1 Kings 8:54), Jesus (Lk 22:39-41), Paul (Acts 20:36) and the early church all prayed while kneeling. One day we will all find ourselves kneeling in worship:

Therefore God also highly exalted him and gave him the name

that is above every name, so that at the name of Jesus every knee should bend, in heaven and on earth and under the earth, and every tongue should confess that Jesus Christ is Lord, to the glory of God the Father. (Phil 2:9-11)

Standing. Standing to pray is also a common prayer posture. Standing is a gesture of respect. We stand in our culture when a judge enters the courtroom and when the our national anthem is sung. When we are seated and a friend approaches, we stand to greet them. In some cultures, people stand when Scripture is read in public. The Israelites stood for three hours as they corporately confessed their sins, and they stood for another three hours as Scripture was read (Neh 9:1-5). Jesus assumed people would be standing for prayer: "Whenever you stand praying, forgive, if you have anything against anyone; so that your Father in heaven may also forgive you your trespasses" (Mk 11:25).

Prostration. Falling on our faces before God is associated with repentance and the most extreme humility, and sometimes despair. Moses and Aaron fell on their faces when the Lord threatened to consume the Israelites (Num 16:43-46). Joshua expressed his despair by falling prostrate (Josh 7:6-7). When David saw the angel of the Lord standing between earth and heaven with a drawn sword stretched out over Jerusalem, David and the elders fell on their faces (1 Chron 21:16).

Lying prostrate isn't always a sign of failure and judgment. Jesus poured out his grief by throwing himself to the ground in the Garden of Gethsemane (Mt 26:38-39). John revealed prostration as a sign of worship, "And all the angels stood around the throne and around the elders and the four living creatures, and they fell on their faces before the throne and worshiped God" (Rev 7:11).

Positioning the hands. We can use our hands in prayer in many ways. One of the oldest prayer postures of the early church is the *orant,* featured in frescoes and in graffiti that decorates the catacombs where early Christians gathered to worship. The arms are at the side of the body with elbows bent. The forearms are horizontal to the ground with the palms up.

There are many ways to use your fingers, hands and arms to assist you in prayer and adoration to God. Solomon stood before the altar of the Lord with his hands spread out to heaven (1 Kings 8:22); the Israelites raised their hands in response to Ezra blessing the Lord (Neh 8:6). At times during prayer I use my hands to cover my face— especially in times of repentance. When the benediction is given, I like to cup my hands near my heart to indicate my desire to receive the blessing from the Lord. In meditation, I like to rest my hands on my legs or knees, palms up, to indicate my openness to the voice of the Holy Spirit. Sometimes I lift my hands expectantly, like a child, during worship. To focus in prayer I may fold my hands or put them palm to palm and place the tops of my fingers to my chin with my head slightly bowed.

Bowing the head. Bowing the head signals respect and submission to the Lord. Abraham's servant bowed his head and worshiped when the Lord answered his prayer for Isaac's wife (Gen 24:12-27). Moses bowed his head when he was in the Lord's presence and asked the Lord to pardon the Israelites' sin (Ex 34:8-9).

Other prayer postures. There are many other ways to use your body in prayer and worship:

- In the Psalms, David spoke of praying in bed (Ps 63:5-6).
- The "sinful" woman bathed Jesus' feet with her tears, kissed them and anointed them with perfume (Lk 7:36-50).

- The repentant tax collector prayed by beating his breast in repentance (Lk 18:13).

- The crowd praised Jesus by waving palm branches and shouting (Mt 21:5-9).

- Jesus looked up to heaven when he prayed (Mk 6:41).

- James encourages praying and anointing the sick with oil (Jas 5:13-14).

At times I pray while I'm running, driving the car or riding my bike. Some people love to pray through singing or painting or dancing. Some people connect with God through prayer while knitting or practicing similar hobbies.

For too long we have ignored the role our bodies play in our Christian formation. Helping youth to see the importance of their bodies for the worship of God is extremely important—especially for adolescents, who are developmentally focused on the body. Teaching and showing our young people how to incorporate the use of their bodies in encounters with God is a significant aspect of presence-centered youth ministry.

THE SIGN OF THE CROSS

Making the sign of the cross has become a part of my spiritual practice, but I first had to overcome the intimidation of the only-Catholics-do-that looks from my friends. Many Protestants hold that "we left this medieval practice behind after the Reformation." But the sign of the cross was around a long time before the medieval period. It was a way for early Christians under persecution to identify each other. Over time it changed from simply outlining a cross on the forehead to the larger gesture from forehead to heart, shoulder to shoulder. Many church fathers, including Cyprian (third century), John Chrysostom (fourth century) and Saint Basil (fourth century), spoke devotionally about the sign of the cross. Tertullian, theologian and author from the second century, writes of the uses of the sign of the cross:

> In all our travels and movements, in all our coming in and going out, in putting on our shoes, at the bath, at the table, in lighting our candles, in lying down, in sitting down, whatever employment occupies us, we mark our foreheads with the sign of the cross.[5]

The sign of the cross was used to communicate theology in early church controversies. A group known as Monophysites used only one finger to make the sign of the cross, drawing attention to their heretical view of the one nature of Christ. Those who believed in the Trinity positioned their fingers to emphasize the Trinity and the (two natures) of Christ.

A careful reading of church history shows that the practice and symbolism of the sign of the cross was not something the Reformers were interested in leaving behind, especially Martin Luther, the father of the Protestant Reformation.

> The sign of the cross is ecumenical, in that it is used by the Orthodox, Roman Catholics, Lutherans, and Episcopalians, and is slowly increasing in use among mainline Protestants.
>
> The sign of the cross is a treasured part of our liturgical heritage as Lutherans, because the practice was encouraged and used by Martin Luther himself. Luther made provisions for using the sign of the cross on at least four occasions.
>
> The text of Luther's 1526 Order of Baptism called for the sign of the cross to be made over the candidate as a part of baptism.

"Receive the sign of the holy cross on both your forehead and your breast" (*Luther's Works,* 53:107).

In his order for the Ordination of Ministers of the Word, Luther says of the benediction: "The ordinator blesses them with the sign of the cross" (*Luther's Works,* 53:126).

Luther instructed his followers to make the sign of the cross at both the beginning and the end of the day as a beginning to daily prayers. In the Small Catechism, in the section on morning and evening prayers, Luther says: "When you get out of bed, bless yourself with the holy cross and say, 'In the name of God, the Father, the Son, and the Holy Spirit. Amen.'" This same instruction is given for bedtime.[6]

Studying the history of the sign of the cross has convinced me that this is another treasured family heirloom that needs to be brought out of the attic, dusted off and reinstituted into our Christian practice. My church ends every Sunday by coming forward to receive the body and blood of our Lord Jesus. I conclude this transcendent experience by making the sign of the cross. I also make the sign of the cross whenever I pray the *Glory Be* or when I pledge to love God with all of my mind, heart, soul and strength.

To make the sign of the cross, I first put the two fingers closest to my thumb together and touch them to the end of my thumb to make a little circle. The three fingers represent the triune God I serve. The circle represents the eternality of God. I put my littlest finger against the finger next to it and let the tips of the two fingers rest on my palm. These two fingers represent the deity and humanity of Jesus Christ.

Once my hand is formed in this symbolic manner, I make the sign of the cross in four quick steps:

- I touch my forehead with the end of my two fingers and thumb and pray, "In the name of the Father."

- I move my hand to the middle of my chest and say, "and of the Son."

- I move my hand to the left side of my chest and I say, "and of the Holy Spirit."

- I move my hand to the right side of my chest and I say, "Amen."

At times I use the most ancient form of the sign of the cross (tracing the form of the cross with two quick strokes of my finger or thumb) on my forehead while committing my mind to the things of God, on my eyes that they would stay focused on Christ, on my mouth that I might glorify God by the words I speak, on my ears that I would listen to the Holy Spirit's still small voice, over my heart, that I would stay true to my calling and nurture a heart of passion for God, on my hands that they would engage in doing the will of God, and on my feet that they would always follow the Lord Jesus. The sign of the cross is another way for me to acknowledge the wonderful grace of God and the sacrifice of Jesus Christ on the cross. It also reminds me to love God with all my heart, soul, mind and strength.

Once again, let me caution you not to teach your entire youth group to begin crossing themselves next Sunday. By all means, I hope you recover these wonderful family heirlooms, but use wisdom and discernment when introducing them to others. Consider incorporating it into your own spiritual practices, waiting until an appropriate opportunity to speak with the pastor and elders in your church community.

PRAYING WITH ICONS

Icons were important visual expressions of Scripture at a time when few Christians were able to read. Praying with icons is another Protestant lightning rod. Most Protestants think that people are praying to the icon, but it is more accurate to say we pray *with* icons, similar to praying with Scripture or praying with the inspiration provided by the handiwork of God's creation.

In his book *Behold the Beauty of the Lord: Praying with Icons*, Henri Nouwen shares his devotional experiences with four icons (which are included in the book as foldouts) and helps us understand what this practice means:

It is easy to become a victim of the vast array of visual stimuli surrounding us. The "powers and principalities" control many of our daily images. Posters, billboards, television, videocassettes, movies and store windows continuously assault our eyes and inscribe their images upon our memories.

Still we do not have to be passive victims of a world that wants to entertain and distract us. We can make some decisions and choices. A spiritual life in the midst of our energy-draining society requires us to take conscious steps to safeguard that inner space where we can keep our eyes fixed on the beauty of the Lord. . . .

Why icons? Would it not have been better to use more accessible paintings such as those by Michelangelo, Rembrandt or Marc Chagall? The great treasures of Western art might indeed be more attractive, but I have chosen icons, because they are created for the sole purpose of offering access, through the gate of the visible, to the mystery of the invisible. Icons are painted to lead us into the inner room of prayer and bring us close to the heart of God.[7]

I have experienced some profound encounters with God while praying with icons. Instead of passing around icons to your youth group for a prayer time, consider taking your youth group to the local art museum and exposing them to the religious paintings and icons there. I've done this several times, setting a designated time for browsing through the religious art section. I instruct students to prayerfully consider each work of art and to be sensitive to what they are drawn to. I encourage them to select a particular piece of art to focus on and meditate with. I remind them to listen carefully to what the Holy Spirit might be saying to them through the work of art. When we gather together, we take time to share what we discovered and what God impressed upon us. Try it. You might be surprised at how your young people respond to this.

KEEPING THE HOURS

The origins of keeping the hours (also called fixed-hour prayer, the daily office of prayer and liturgy of the hours) are rooted in ancient Judaism. The psalmist declared, "Seven times a day I praise you for your righteous ordinances" (Ps 119:164). We are told in the book of Daniel, "Daniel . . . continued to go to his house, which had windows in its upper room open toward Jerusalem, and to get down on his knees three times a day to pray to his God and praise him" (Dan 6:10). Daniel was practicing fixed-hour prayer as any faithful Hebrew would do.

In the early church we see fixed-hour prayer continuing when the disciples gathered on the day of Pentecost for prayer at nine in the morning, the time for third-hour prayer (Acts 2:15); when Peter and John go "to the temple at the hour of prayer, at three o'clock in the afternoon" (Acts 3:1); and shortly before Peter and Cornelius met for the first time, Peter went up on the roof to pray at noon (Acts 10:9).

Early church fathers wrote and spoke of fixed-hour prayer as an integral characteristic of Christianity. Keeping the hours has continued to our present day, although many branches of Protestantism have misplaced or forgotten the wonderful history of this practice. However, Christians from all branches of Christianity are rediscovering this ancient family heirloom.

The beauty of the prayers and liturgy along with the rhythm of keeping the hours has been a key part of my own Christian practice and formation. It has also been a key part of the programming, in various forms, at all the YouthFront camps. A typical day at one of the camps looks like this:

- First thing in the morning is a twelve-minute office, which includes a liturgical reading and response, prayer, the Apostles' Creed, a contemplative song, Scripture reading, silence and a closing prayer.

- After breakfast, time is allotted for solitude in one of seventy sacred spaces spread out over six hundred acres.

- Before lunch the whole camp gathers for midday prayer, which is similar to but longer than morning prayer. Midday is overwhelmingly the favorite part of the campers' experience.

> I like midday mainly because of the time of day it happens. Lunchtime is when I would set my course either toward or away from God. Midday is a great way for me to pause, reflect on God's character and invite him into everything I do throughout the rest of the day.
>
> **NICK, COLLEGE STUDENT**

- Before retiring is Compline, which takes about as long as morning prayer. This is a time to use liturgy, prayer and Scripture appropriate to the end of the day.

The YouthFront staff also gathers every day for midday prayer. This has become an integral part of who we are as a community of youth workers. Youth pastors and others occasionally drop by to join us in midday prayer. It serves as a wonderful reminder that our most important work is nurturing our own relationship with

God and acknowledging that God is at the center of what we are about.

Phyllis Tickle, an extraordinary author and contributing editor of religion for *Publishers Weekly,* has made a wonderful contribution to my spiritual practice and to my daily rhythm of practicing the presence of God. Tickle has organized prayers from the *Book of Common Prayer* and other sources into a contemporary fixed-hour prayer guide called *The Divine Hours.* It's a three-volume work— *Prayers for Summertime, Prayers for Autumn and Wintertime* and *Prayers for Spring.* Fixed-hour prayers start with morning prayer (6 to 9 a.m.), followed by midday prayer (11 a.m. to 2 p.m.) and evening prayer (5 to 8 p.m.), and ends with Compline at bedtime. The amount of time for the prayers depends on the prayer (usually five to fifteen minutes). Tickle writes in the introduction of *The Divine Hours:*

> Christians today, wherever they practice the discipline of fixed-hour prayer, frequently find themselves filled with a conscious awareness that they are handing their worship, at its final "Amen," on to other Christians in the next time zone. Like relay runners passing a lighted torch, those who do the work of fixed-hour prayer do create thereby a continuous cascade of praise before the throne of God. . . .
>
> *The Divine Hours* are prayers of praise offered as a sacrifice of thanksgiving and faith to God and as a sweet-smelling incense of the human soul before the throne of God. To offer them is to serve before that throne as part of the priesthood of all believers. It is to assume the "office" of attendant upon the Divine.[8]

Several years ago I discovered a website, <www.SacredSpace.ie>, started by a small group of Jesuits in Dublin, Ireland, led by Father

Alan McGuckian. Every day a new prayer exercise is featured. This site became a special place to join with thousands of others around the world for contemplative prayer.

Several youth workers and I expressed our appreciation for their site and asked them to partner with us to create a site for adolescents. They perceived that our being Protestants "was a really good thing." Within a few weeks I was in Dublin working out the details of this partnership. The big question I had was whether they would allow us to adjust the content for Protestant users. Father Alan responded, "Absolutely. You have to. We just want to help people pray." The result is <www.SacredGateway.org>. Check it out as another resource for your prayer practices.

Keeping the hours not only connects us with other Christians around the world who are praying, but it also connects us with the big story of God and his people who have been praying these prayers for thousands of years.

LORD, TEACH US TO PRAY

Make these prayer practices a part of your Christian experience and see how they impact your relationship with God before you introduce them to your kids. Even better, connect with a small community of friends, church members or fellow youth workers and put some of these prayer exercises to practice among yourselves. These practices are for *you*. Only consider introducing these practices to your youth when you have used them and understand them enough to explain them.

The prayer practices we have looked at are not an exhaustive list, not even close. I didn't discuss common practices such as intercessory prayer, public prayer, dedicatory prayer, praying Scripture, singing prayers, prayer walks, prophetic prayer and others.

Jesus disciples' approached their master with a request "Lord, teach us to pray" (Lk 11:1). We can make the same request and also ask for the willingness to spend a lifetime learning how to commune with God along with instilling the same passion in the youth we work with.

NINE

Using Scripture in Presence-Centered Youth Ministry

s it possible for young people to fall in love with Scripture? Can we help them hunger for the story of God at work among God's people? The answer is yes!

Part of the solution is for *us* to fall in love with Scripture. We can cultivate a passion for it, seeing Scripture as a living, sacred text. We can nurture communities that will engage with each other in a truthful examination of the Bible. We can trust the Holy Spirit to speak to us and those in our communities through Scripture.

We can also resist attempts to domesticate the Holy Spirit and dumb down the text. Most teenagers view the Bible as boring. Most adults do too if they are honest. I am convinced that this is the result of approaching it as a science book or a book of facts and propositions instead of as a sacred text that is the primary medium through which the Spirit of God reveals truth to us.

In seminary I was taught to dissect and open up a verse, phrase, word or even a part of a word in order to get at what God "really means to say." It was up to me to use my reason to discover the truth contained in the text. Henry Knight addresses this experience:

While well intentioned, the apologetic strategies of evangelical theology have conceded too much to modernity at the outset. Their success in convincing those steeped in modernity of the truth of historic Christianity has been marginal, and they have reassured the faithful at the cost of reinforcing the rationalist claims of the Enlightenment, which should have been challenged. As a result, they have permitted the autonomous rational human agent, biblical text in hand, to supplant the agency of the Holy Spirit as the interpreter of Scripture, who leads us into all truth (Jn 16:12).[1]

READING THE BIBLE DEVOTIONALLY

How we view Scripture is a controversial issue in the modern-postmodern evangelical debate. One of the core problems is the failure to understand the difference between reading and studying Scripture cognitively and devotionally. Both are important and necessary for our Christian formation, but they are distinct from each other.

A cognitive approach to Scripture involves reading and studying the Bible exegetically—thinking, evaluating, synthesizing data, reasoning and giving attention to language, symbols and context. We read Scripture cognitively to comprehend the meaning of the text through developed study methods, called hermeneutics (from a Greek verb meaning "to interpret"). The goal of reading Scripture cognitively is to analyze the text so we understand the intent of the original author. This is done by examining the original languages, understanding the historical and cultural contexts, interpretation principles and other theological considerations.

While this approach to reading Scripture is essential, I'm concerned by the overly confident attitude that we can incontrovertibly get at the "objective" original meaning of the text with absolute certainty. The complexity of language and other communication variables makes it difficult to understand objectively what your spouse said two minutes ago, let alone what someone wrote two thousand years ago. And yet we must try to understand what the original intent was and is.

At the same time we must embrace epistemological humility when it comes to how much certainty we hold. More theologians are calling for an approach to Scripture not only with hermeneutical tools in hand, but also the guidance of the Holy Spirit within the context of a community of believers.

A devotional or inspirational reading of Scripture is quite different from a cognitive reading. The purpose of a devotional reading of Scripture is to encounter God. The focus is on listening for the Holy Spirit to speak to us through Scripture.

Devotional and inspirational Scripture reading has been neglected in evangelical youth ministry. Presence-centered youth ministry is impossible without Scripture at the core of your ministry philosophy and praxis. George Gallup Jr. writes in *The Next American Spirituality,*

When I speak of young people reading Scripture as Sacred Text, I am not saying that it is unimportant for us to teach our youth hermeneutical principles that will enable them [to] rightly discern the Scripture. Indeed, young people will increasingly shy away from lectures or monologues. They want to participate in the discovery of truth, not simply be presented with it in finished form.[2]

THE BIBLE AS SACRED TEXT

No matter how aware you are of the dialogue concerning Scripture and truth, you are surely cognizant of the attraction that adolescents have for narrative. Stories that convey the truth of God at work in creation; of God at work among humanity; and the stories of what God has done through history are more quickly embraced by young people than sterile propositionalism. Our youth are fascinated with the mystery of God and God's work throughout the cosmos. We don't have to be afraid that the latest scientific discovery is going to finally discredit the Bible. Scripture contains narrative, poems, songs, parables, metaphors, history, principles, propositions, laws, philosophy, commands, mystery, confessions, sex, intrigue, love plus much more.

I have been introducing young people to the Bible as sacred text, teaching them how to read it differently, teaching them how to experience the depth and richness of all that is there. Instead of reading the Bible for quantity I show them how to read it qualitatively. I teach them to enter into it as the narrative of God working among his people and explain to them that they are a continuation of the story of God. I emphasize the role of the Holy Spirit in listening to God speak through Scripture. I stress the importance of reading and discerning Scripture in connection with a community of believers.

Presence-centered youth ministry engages in the Christian formation of youth by equipping them to study the Bible cognitively *and* devotionally in order to experience the presence of God. Many resources are available that explain how to exegete Scripture, so I'll limit further comments to devotional reading and interaction with Scripture.

Richard Hays of Duke Divinity School suggests that we need to use our imaginations to recover the art of reading Scripture.[3] He believes reading Scripture as an art form is difficult. We don't just decide to be artists and begin making masterpieces overnight. As artists must develop their skills, so we must develop the skills of reading Scripture. Hays believes beauty is the goal of interpreting Scripture and that Jewish believers have always embraced the reading of sacred text as the most complex and powerful art form. He mentions several points about reading Scripture:

- Scripture has multiple complex senses.

- We are called to a conversion of the imagination as we read.

- A unified story thread runs through from Genesis to Revelation.

- Scripture, the story of God, is open-ended; therefore we should enter into the story as a reader.

- Scripture must be read in communities of prayer, worship, service and mission.

Rugged individualism, a key component of Enlightenment thinking linked with the pursuit of happiness, is the fuel for modern democracy, capitalism and technological and cultural progress. Rationalism views the center of moral values as in the individual. And yet Scripture is not directed to individuals but to communities of people. The church of Jesus Christ is established upon the revelation of God to his people. God has revealed himself through creation, through events in history, through Jesus Christ and through Scripture. This has resulted in people gathering into communities of believers who embrace the revelation of God. Out of these communities of God's people have come tradition and the development of a way of life that perpetuates the ongoing story of God at work among his people.

As members of God's community of faith, we continue to act out this drama of the ages, the unfolding of the story of God at work among his people. In community we remember our heritage and traditions; we read Scripture and pray together to discern the voice of the Holy Spirit; we worship, dialogue with one another and live missionally to faithfully serve God.

Gallup believes reading Scripture in community and in connection with God's metanarrative is essential, especially for young people who are hungry for authentic stories of redemption. He writes:

> Sermons and other forms of communication need to be soaked . . . in the great story. But increasingly important to allowing truth to "take" in the postmodern consciousness will require incorporating the preacher's own experiences, and the lived experiences of others. And such stories, when they become a vehicle for conveying truth in sermons and other writings, should avoid being too tidy, too moralistic.[4]

We should be responsive to Paul's instruction: "Until I arrive, give attention to the public reading of Scripture, to exhorting, to teaching" (1 Tim 4:13). Attention to a public—or communal—reading of Scripture should be an integral part of our youth ministries. One way this is accomplished is by having the youth read the text together aloud. You may find it helpful to print copies of the text or project it so everyone can read the same translation.

Reading and interacting with the text should result in Spirit-led exhortation and teaching, an essential part of connecting your youth to the big story of God and helping them see themselves in the ongoing narrative of God. Presence-centered youth ministry, while not neglecting a cognitive reading of the Scripture, will incorporate devotional reading as a core practice.

Devotional reading of Scripture is an important corrective to the overemphasis of cognitive reading focused primarily on a propositional understanding of Scripture.

I'm not discounting the importance of propositions but the overextension of modern propositionalism. Alister McGrath places the value of cognitive reading in its appropriate context:

Any view of revelation which regards God's self-disclosure as the mere transmission of facts concerning God is seriously deficient. To reduce revelation to principles and concepts is to suppress the element of mystery, holiness and wonder to God's self-disclosure. "First principles" may enlighten and inform; they do not force us to our knees in reverence and awe.[5]

STORYTELLING

The first step in overcoming young people's view that the Bible is boring is to help them see Scripture as story. Everyone's ears perk up when someone says, "I have a story for you." Telling stories pulls the listener in. It should be no different when we communicate stories from Scripture.

Encourage storytelling among your youth. Storytelling is an art to be developed. Helping your youth tell, listen to and interpret stories will build community among your group and will equip them to engage more fully with Scripture.

You can also create opportunities for them to act out the stories, write about the stories, and paint or draw the stories. Create space for them to meditate on the stories from Scripture, dialogue about their understanding of the stories and paraphrase stories into a contemporary context.

You can also use novels, movies and musicals that retell biblical stories. The 1999 miniseries *Jesus* is an excellent resource that fires the imagination and offers a powerful telling of the story of Christ.[6]

SACRED READING

Reading Scripture aloud to our young people is important. Instead of reading isolated verses, read an entire passage with its broader context. Reading and using Scripture liturgically, with responsive reading along with periods of silence to allow for reflection is another way for youth to interact with the Bible. Help students memorize Scripture, such as Psalm 23, to equip them for group prayer.

Reading Scripture as a way to come into the presence of God was practiced in Old Testament times. Jewish believers communed with God by gathering for the reading of Scripture.

> All the people gathered together into the square before the Water Gate. They told the scribe Ezra to bring the book of the law of Moses, which the LORD had given to Israel. . . . He read from it facing the square before the Water Gate from early morning until midday, in the presence of the men and the women and those who could understand; and the ears of all the people were attentive to the book of the law. . . . And Ezra opened the book in the sight of all the people, for he was standing above all the people; and when he opened it, all the people stood up. Then Ezra blessed the LORD, the great God, and all the people answered, "Amen, Amen," lifting up their hands. Then they bowed their heads and worshiped the LORD with their faces to the ground. (Neh 8:1, 3, 5-7)

Approaching Scripture for the purpose of encountering the presence of God has continued to the present day, although it has been neglected by many branches of Protestantism. It's being rediscovered as a primary practice of Christian formation. In the introduction of *Take and Read,* Eugene Peterson writes:

> Spiritual reading, designated lectio divina by our ancestors, has fallen on bad times. It has always been a prized arrow in the quiver of those determined to cultivate a God-aware life, but has suffered a severe blunting in our century. . . . Reading today

is largely a consumer activity—people devour books, magazines, pamphlets, and newspapers for information that will fuel their ambition or careers or competence. The faster the better, the more the better. . . . Spiritual reading is mostly a lover's activity—a dalliance with words, reading as much between the lines as in the lines themselves.[7]

LECTIO DIVINA

The word *lectio* is Latin for "reading" and is derived from the Latin word *lego*, which describes gathering and harvesting. The word *divina* is Latin for "divine." Lectio divina is a divine reading of Scripture, either individually or in community, with a desire to enter into the presence of God and to follow the Holy Spirit's prompting through a process of meditation, prayer and contemplation. The purpose is to hear from God through Scripture resulting in enlightenment and a response of obedience and devotion.

Before beginning lectio divina, pray. Our prayer is a part of the process that centers our focus upon God, stills our hearts and minds, and acknowledges that we expect to interact with the Holy Spirit through Scripture.

Next, select a text to read, by following a lectionary or other Bible reading plan or by selecting a text randomly. Several resources are available on the Internet with Scripture reading suggestions.

Slowly and thoughtfully read the text, out loud, if possible. Be alert to the manner in which the Holy Spirit uses the text to penetrate your heart. Allow God to speak to you, to draw your attention to something in the text. If you sense the Holy Spirit illuminating a particular portion of the text, a phrase or word, allow the meaning or stirring to resonate within you.

Meditate—reflect intently—on the portion of Scripture you sense the Holy Spirit is drawing you to. Meditation also has to do with a careful and disciplined listening in the midst of reflection. One profound change that can happen through meditation is a new understanding of Scripture. The Holy Spirit actively illuminates Scripture and speaks to the person who passionately places himself or herself in the presence of God to listen.

When I am reading and meditating on Scripture and experience the Holy Spirit speaking specifically to me out of the text, Hebrews 4:12 often comes to mind: "Indeed, the word of God is living and active, sharper than any two-edged sword, piercing until it divides soul from spirit, joints from marrow; it is able to judge the thoughts and intentions of the heart." Saint Jerome highlights the way that the Holy Spirit can speak different specific messages to us through the same Scriptures:

> In the field of the Scripture multicolored flowers, ready for the picking, are to be found everywhere. Every species is present there, red roses, white lilies and flowers of every color: there is an embarrassment of riches. It remains for us but to collect the flowers which seem to us the most beautiful. And if we gather up roses we should not be unhappy that we have not picked lilies; and if we have gathered lilies, we are not disdaining the humble violets. All is beautiful and fascinating in the sweet land promised to generous souls who have agreed to labor a little among the holy books.[8]

Think about how many times you have read a specific Scripture without noticing a particular thought before. We are transformed when we hear from the Holy Spirit!

As the Holy Spirit illuminates Scripture, it is our responsibility (if we are reading privately) to respond appropriately. If we are engaged in lectio divina in community, we process together what the Holy Spirit may be saying to us. To honestly interact with Scripture means that we are willing to embrace whatever God is saying to us. Confession and repentance are often appropriate responses.

Contemplation is also an important part of a sacred reading. Dwelling in God's presence, we contemplate how Scripture should impact our attitudes, actions and behavior. Take time to *be*. Be with God. Be with the text. Be honest. Be obedient. Be enveloped in the grace and love of God. Be still. Be in peace. Allow the Holy Spirit to help you truly *be*.

I recommend keeping a journal of your encounters with the Holy Spirit in the midst of reading and meditating on Scripture. Encourage young people to try journaling and help them begin the process. Use those journals to share life with each other. Engaging one other in this way is sacramental and binds us together in the presence of the divine.

I have recently become involved in a missional leadership project. A group of theologians and leaders have been working together for a decade, doing deep theological work concerning ecclesiology. Part of their rule of life is the practice of *dwelling in the Word*. Every time they gather (which is often), they read aloud Luke 10:1-12, the story of Jesus' appointment of seventy disciples to go on a mission. After they slowly read the text, they dwell in the Scripture, listening in quiet solitude for the Holy Spirit to speak to them individually. When their time of silence is complete they pair up to share what they sensed from the Holy Spirit. Then the whole group reconvenes, and each person shares what they heard from their partner. This ten-year practice has proved to them the organic, living nature of Scripture that continues to yield new and powerful truth.

Helping young people interact with Scripture encourages them to approach Scripture in new ways that will alter their Scripture-is-boring mindset. Lectio divina isn't an excuse to ignore the importance of a cognitive understanding of Scripture. Isaac of Stella in the twelfth century wrote of bringing the two approaches together: "Keep the solicitude of Martha without losing the devotion of Mary."

When we're passionate about presence-centered youth ministry, we'll be committed to imparting cognitive and devotional Scripture reading to young people. Scripture is a primary tool for spiritual transformation and will enable youth to develop an obsession for encountering God's presence.

TEN

A Rule of Life

I f you're anything like me, you don't even like the word *rule*. My overall reaction toward it is negative. I don't like rules most of the time. However, when I say *rule of life*, I think very positive thoughts.

A rule of life is an intention to place Jesus Christ at the center of life, ministry and community. It serves to train us in the ways of Jesus and to remind us who is Lord of our lives. We can view a rule of life as a tool for shaping our Christian formation and leading us into a deeper relationship with Christ and with others. A rule of life can also give shape to our daily lives, not in a rigid way, but in a life-giving way.

A rule of life means embracing certain values and practices for one's spiritual formation. It should provide structure for many areas of our lives—prayer, Scripture, fellowship, worship, sabbath, mission, justice, service, sacraments, work, social justice, friendship, rest, nutrition, exercise, creativity, giving and so on.

Some parts of a rule of life may be observed daily, others weekly, some monthly, while other aspects of a rule of life may be annual events. An effective rule of life should not feel like a burden but should set us free to be who God intended us to be in a loving and authentic relationship with him.

IT ALL BEGAN WHEN . . .

Ben grew up in a Christian home and was sent by his parents to attend an expensive college in a major city. It wasn't long before Ben became disgusted with the decadence of big-city college life. He soon left for a quieter place to focus on his relationship with God. Before long several friends gathered around Ben, drawn to his spirituality. They asked Ben to help them grow in Christ. Ben set out to disciple his friends by establishing an environment for a disciplined spiritual life. However, his friends weren't ready for Ben's passionate pursuit of Christ. In fact, they eventually tried to poison him.

You may have figured out that Ben is Benedict of Nursia who lived in sixth-century Italy. Benedict escaped and for a time reflected on what Christian formation should be about. Eventually Benedict, determined not to fail again in developing disciples for Jesus Christ, established over a dozen monasteries. He wrote a rule of life to govern the communities in Christian formation, building upon the traditions of Anthony of the Desert and Pachomius, It contained rules for living in community but also allowed for individual differences that weren't to the detriment of the whole. The mix of discipline and compassion that characterized Benedict's rule of life has been used as a model for others for fifteen hundred years.

In chapter seven we reviewed David's encounter with Goliath. David selected five smooth stones out of the brook to use with his slingshot. The stones and his pouch, slingshot and staff were the few tools David the shepherd used to accomplish what God had called him to.

A rule of life is formed around values and practices. You might include values such as stability, hospitality, community, fidelity, mission, obedience, stewardship, simplicity and learning. You might include practices concerning prayer, Scripture reading, study, fasting, retreats, pilgrimages, exercise, the Eucharist, spiritual direction and examination.

You can be like David and utilize specific tools that work for you. Develop a rule of life that equips and enables you to do what God has called you to.

DEVELOPING YOUR RULE OF LIFE

To begin developing a rule of life, start with something basic and simple. You can always add to your rule along the way. For reference, let's consider two examples: a basic rule of life and a more developed one.

A simple rule of life might look something like this:

I submit to a rule of life of stability, fidelity, community and simplicity. I will seek to live out this rule of life by ordering my life around the principles that flow out of these values.

The spiritual practices that I will incorporate into my rule of life will be consistent Scripture reading (four to five times per week) using a variety of methods to interact with the text, including lectio divina, meditation and following the lectionary.

I will engage in prayer daily, using a variety of prayer practices (imaginative prayer, respiratory prayer, praying Scripture, intercessory prayer, etc.). I will practice the discipline of study by reading at least five hours per week. I will spend at least three hours per week studying a portion of Scripture or a theological subject.

I will go on at least one retreat a year for a minimum of two days.

Over time a rule of life can develop into something more advanced:

I submit to a rule of life of stability, fidelity, community, simplicity and learning. I will strive to live out this rule of life by ordering my life around the principles that flow out of these values. I desire to exercise my faith so that I may be formed as a follower of Jesus. I will embrace spiritual practices that will help me live in the presence of God.

The spiritual practices I will incorporate into my rule of life will be consistent Scripture reading (four to five times per week) using a variety of methods to interact with the text. I will dwell in particular passages of Scripture for extended periods of time.

I will engage in daily prayer, using a variety of prayer practices (imaginative prayer, respiratory prayer, praying Scripture, intercessory prayer, etc.). I will take seriously the admonition of Paul to pray without ceasing.

I will practice the discipline of study by reading at least seven hours per week. I will spend at least three hours per week studying theology.

I will go on at least three retreats a year for a minimum of two days per retreat. I will take an annual pilgrimage.

I will engage in regular spiritual direction.

I will engage in fasting at least once a month.

I will exercise my body at least four times per week and will limit myself to eating fast food no more than three times per month.

I will engage in tangible acts of hospitality at least twice a week.

I will strive to enjoy works of beauty, such as music, films, art, architecture and poetry, on a regular basis.

I will continue to date my wife on a weekly basis.

I will consciously seek to view my life holistically, doing all things to the glory of God.

VALUES

In Christian history the following values were generally included in religious vows. These values are once again being considered seriously by a generation of young people who are burned out by materialism and nihilism and who are looking for a way to be more missionally related to their culture and the world they live in.

Stability. In church history, stability formed the basis of the monastic vow. Those entering a monastic community committed to grow in Christ among people they would live and die with. The parish model, church within a community for a lifetime, that has existed throughout most of Christianity is the antithesis of the North American church phenomenon of church hopping.

We live in a mobile culture. We have also gone crazy with an ethos of consumerism. We love our freedom to choose what suits us best. If we don't like the service we get at this store, another one is across the street. If we don't like the way things are going at our church, seven others are within five blocks.

The modern concept of individualism, which has added a lot of good things to our lifestyles, has also left us disconnected and lacking much that brings health to our lives. The Christian faith is built on community, starting with the triune God. Scripture was written mostly to communities instead of individuals. Our communities, with their positives and negatives, are an essential part of our Christian formation and pilgrimage of faith.

I remember as a young youth worker hearing a message about learning difficult life lessons by staying put. My first youth ministry mentor, Al Metsker, drilled into me that giving up because of conflict and moving on only results in needing to take the test over again. Some people spend their whole lives in that cycle.

After three decades of youth ministry in the same organization, I have seen the wonderful benefits of stability. Working with the teenagers of the teenagers I worked with earlier in my ministry is fulfilling. Just about everywhere I go around town, I see people who have been involved in our ministry. Rarely do I go into a coffee shop without having a conversation with someone who came to camp or went on a mission trip or had some other youth ministry connection with me.

There are obviously times and situations when moving on is being obedient to the Holy Spirit. However, the Holy Spirit is cited way too often as the reason for moving on, when, in fact, the Holy Spirit had nothing to do with it. Churches and youth ministries constantly in transition from one pastor to another are hard pressed to form deep communities of transformation.

Benedict believed that a monk who entered the monastery was coming there to live his entire life and to die there. What would our churches and youth ministries look like if we took stability seriously?

Fidelity. Fidelity speaks of faithfulness and allegiance and is an essential value for youth workers who embrace presence-centered youth ministry. Fidelity is an important component we bring into our relationship with Jesus Christ. A rule of life helps us pursue personal piety and a lifestyle of holiness.

My wife, Vicki, and I recently celebrated our thirtieth anniversary. She's the only woman that I have ever been with. My desire is for that to be true on the day I take my last breath. Fidelity is not only a gift that my wife and I give to each other but also an obedience we bring to Christ and a gift we give to our children, youth and others we live among.

Simplicity. A commitment to simplicity in a rule of life involves the persistent protection of our souls from the busyness of life. Chronic busyness works to make us less than human. Simplicity allows us to focus on what is most important in life by keeping a schedule that isn't overwhelming. Simplicity keeps our most important priorities uncluttered. A commitment to simplicity means we reserve energy for spiritual practices. Simplicity covers the importance of living within our financial means and not overextending ourselves financially. Avoiding debt is essential to living in the freedom of God.

Some view simplicity as a watered down version of the vow of poverty, but I disagree. Simplicity is a commitment to a lifetime exploration of what is enough, what is a need versus a want, how we can order our lives to be more generous, and how to avoid the consumeristic values of our culture. Simplicity will continually form us and nurture our commitment to presence-centered youth ministry.

Community. Our community is where we work with each other to be formed spiritually, where we encourage each other to resist temptations such as unbridled consumerism and selfish living. It's within our community life that we flesh out what it means to live missionally. When we live in community, we are accountable for the way we live. Adopting a rule of life that focuses on the importance of community not only addresses a core human need of belonging and feeling accepted but also responds to a primary Christian virtue of caring for and loving one another. Being closely connected in community with others is instrumental to how we view our church experience, how we pray, how we hear the Holy Spirit and how we read Scripture.

While living a rule of life individually can be a positive aspect of your walk with Christ, a rule of life is designed to be connected to community. Having a group of people that we are experiencing life with, formed around a rule of life, has been at the core of vibrant Christianity for two thousand years. Strong community makes many of the other values in a rule of life—such as stability, fidelity and simplicity—possible.

Proximity. Embracing community involves not only stability but should also explore proximity. The essential nature of a community is connected to physical nearness. This is an increasingly important issue when we want to develop a close-knit fellowship of people in an individualistic culture on the move. It is not uncommon for people to commute thirty miles to go to church. How does that work with the biblical concept of church? Is it possible to be in a church community that is sprawled all over a metropolitan area?

What can we do to rediscover proximity to each other as vitally important to "doing life together"? Right now my wife and I are in the midst of a major transition with our home location because of our desire to place a higher priority on proximity with our church community. We as youth workers should have communities that not only include young people but also adults who are passionately pursuing authentic relationships with Jesus Christ.

The idea that community is our best apologetic is increasingly important in the materialistic and mobile culture we live in. When Jesus tells his disciples all people "will know that you are my disciples, if you have love for one another" (Jn 13:35), we show our love for one another in ways that are appealing to non-Christians and may bring them closer to Christ.

Learning. More than anything else, learning is about nurturing a healthy curiosity—a curiosity that rises out of a passion for the creative God we love. Learning keeps us from becoming rigid or comfortable with the status quo, so it nurtures openness to grace and openness to obedience when God speaks. We serve a God who is on the move, a God who is eager to teach us new things on a journey that is not about settling in or getting by or being comfortable.

For learning about wisdom and instruction, for understanding

words of insight, for gaining instruction in wise dealing, right-
eousness, justice, and equity; to teach shrewdness to the simple, knowledge and prudence to the young—Let the wise also
hear and gain in learning, and the discerning acquire skill, to
understand a proverb and a figure, the words of the wise and
their riddles. The fear of the LORD is the beginning of knowledge; fools despise wisdom and instruction. (Prov 1:2-7)

Some education is formal: college or seminary courses, community classes and conferences, for example. But informal education is
also important. Some of the ways you can create a learning environment include reading from a broad spectrum of genres, watching
documentaries and engaging in robust dialogues.

PRACTICES

After choosing a set of core values to embrace, the next step is discern
which practices (sometimes called spiritual disciplines) will enable
you to uphold your values and live a life of obedience and passion for
Christ. Practices help you to be attuned to what God is saying to you
and help form you spiritually.

Prayer. There are no right or wrong ways to incorporate prayer
into your rule of life. You're building practices to help you to be cognizant of the presence of God. Prayer is a mix of simplicity and complexity but is essential for presence-centered youth ministry, for being conformed to the likeness of Christ and being a minister of God,
serving from a passionate heart and wholeness of soul.

We've already examined a variety of prayer practices—silence and
solitude, imaginative prayer, respiratory prayer, prayer ropes, praying with icons, keeping fixed-hour prayer and others. We shouldn't
neglect intercessory prayer and praying publicly with others. There

are prayer walks, praying Scripture, singing prayers and on and on. I encourage you to try all types of prayer.

Some of these forms of prayer you may want to include in your primary, daily practice of prayer. I use a prayer rope consistently to aid me in intercessory prayer along with daily praying the Lord's Prayer, Psalm 23, the *Glory Be* and my confession of the Apostles' Creed. Fixed-hour prayer, especially midday is a part of my rule of life.

Other forms of prayer you may practice only periodically. For example, I use imaginative prayer and silence and solitude on my semi-annual spiritual retreats. I try to incorporate most of the prayer practices I've mentioned during various seasons of the year.

You may connect some types of prayer to other aspects of your rule of life, for example taking a prayer walk during a retreat or praying with icons on a pilgrimage.

Scripture. Reading, studying, memorizing and meditating on passages from Scripture are also valuable components of a rule of life that help us approach Scripture not only for information and knowledge but for the illumination into our lives that the Holy Spirit brings to us.

I can't emphasize enough the importance of not only reading the Scripture cognitively (exegetically) but also devotionally. Studying the Bible—both the Old and New Testament—through developed methodologies of study is very important. The methods and theories used for cognitive study include examining the original languages, exploring the historical and cultural context, employing principles of interpretation and giving due consideration to theological issues. The goal of reading, thinking, evaluating, synthesizing data, reasoning and giving attention to language, symbols and context in the text is so that the intent of the passage is understood. Jesus was an ardent student of the Scripture.

As I point out elsewhere in this book, however, we must learn to read Scripture devotionally—as Sacred Text—as well, giving careful attention to the illumination and whispers of the Holy Spirit's application to our lives. This aspect of reading Scripture is often neglected or not even considered.

Many portions of Scripture refer to reading and meditating daily on Scripture. There are many variations of Scripture reading as a practice. Some people read a psalm or a proverb every day. Some people follow a lectionary schedule (these are easily found online). Some read through the Bible every year; others dwell in specific passages for an extended period of time. Like the practice of prayer with all its variations, so too, the practice of Scripture reading can take on many forms.

Fasting. Fasting is another practice of Christianity that seems to have largely disappeared over the last century, but it's making a comeback. We see fasting as a spiritual practice throughout Scripture. It's used to create space for discerning the will of the Lord, for confession of sin, to intercede, to pray for healing and restoration.

Fasting is a reminder that we are embodied souls. Our bodies are very much a part of our spirituality. Fasting helps us discipline our bodies and enables us, with the physical reminder of hunger pains, to focus on our spiritual being. Fasting helps us realize that we don't have to give in to the demands of our bodies unwillingly.

Some people include a weekly twenty-four-hour fast within their rule of life, others a monthly or an annual fast. Still others include fasting when certain criteria (a Lenten practice or a major life decision) call for it. As with the other practices, if you include fasting in your rule of life, how you do it is up to you.

Study. If you've been called into youth ministry, study should be an important part of nurturing your vocation and thus a part of your rule of life. The core value at the heart of study is learning. I've heard youth workers boast about not reading a book since they left college or seminary. Even though books like *Wild at Heart* and *Blue Like Jazz* are challenging and enjoyable, consider picking up classics like these:

- *On the Incarnation* by Athanasius
- *The Confessions of Saint Augustine*
- "The First Letter of Clement to the Corinthians" a commentary by Saint Clement
- *The Imitation of Christ* by Thomas à Kempis
- *The Practice of the Presence of God* by Brother Lawrence
- *A Plain Account of Christian Perfection* by John Wesley

My life and ministry would be different without great works like

- *The Moral Vision of the New Testament* by Richard Hays
- *Mere Christianity* by C. S. Lewis
- *The Crucified God* by Jürgen Moltmann
- *Exclusion and Embrace* by Miroslav Volf
- *The Divine Conspiracy* by Dallas Willard
- *The Resurrection of the Son of God* by N. T. Wright

Presence-centered youth ministers should continue to study their vocation. We should be reading books about youth ministry, and because youth ministry is a theological endeavor, we would do well also to feed on a steady diet of theological works.

Journaling. Keeping a journal is something that many people incorporate into their rule of life for the purpose of examining, reviewing and evaluating their experiences and the ways that they see God at work.

A simple way to get started with journaling is to write down Scripture verses that are meaningful and explain why they are important to you. Later you can record events of your day and your feelings about what happened to you. Write about daily consolations and desolations. I write down quotations from books, lines from movies and lyrics from songs. I keep a record of experiences when I sense the Holy Spirit is speaking to me through Scripture, events, prayer or friends.

You don't need to become paralyzed by trying to write in an eloquent style. Writing spontaneously, as the thoughts come, keeps you from getting stuck. You will become more observant about your thoughts and feelings and what is happening around you as you develop your skill in journaling. It's not as easy to rationalize when you write about your life. Many of David's Psalms seem like journal entries to me, recording deep and honest questions and reflections about life and God.

Journaling can help maintain an awareness or even a discovery of our spiritual formation. We develop a higher level of honesty with ourselves. Keeping a journal enables us to become more in tune with our own heart and God's presence in our life.[1]

Sabbath rest. While keeping the sabbath is considered an Old Testament practice, it is certainly a positive thing to set aside a day to acknowledge the freedom we have in Christ. The concept of sabbath rest is being considered by more followers of Jesus as an important part of Christian formation.

In *Keeping the Sabbath Wholly,* Marva Dawn recommends a sabbath rest that allows for meaningful fellowship with family and friends, church attendance, inspirational reading, solitude, sleep, recreation, music, good food and enjoying God's creation.

Sabbath rest is a way to counter a crazy life of materialism and enter into a rhythm of life that celebrates the goodness and richness of life in God. Sabbath rest should include not only physical and spiritual rest but also emotional rest.

When I speak of sabbath rest, I'm not focusing specifically on Saturday or Sunday; I'm referring to the principle of enacting the eschatological rest promised by God. If we're going to engage in presence-centered youth ministry, we should take seriously this spiritual practice. Sabbath rest is an act of humility and worship that reminds us that our ministries are not about us working harder and harder to build a significant youth ministry. God will do the work.

Retreat. In the Gospels we see Jesus taking time to get away. This seems to be a rhythm that he engages in for the purpose of being with his Father.

A retreat allows us to recharge, rest and create space to be with Jesus. Taking a retreat on a regular basis—perhaps two to six times per year—is important for nurturing a spirituality that enables us to lead presence-centered youth ministries. The length of a retreat can be two to three days or longer. Taking a retreat with others can be wonderful but you should also go occasionally by yourself.

There are so many retreat centers today that it isn't hard to find great places to get away to. I recommend finding one or two places you can count on for retreats. I frequent the Conception Abbey, north of Kansas City. I'm familiar enough with it that I know what the schedule is, where the quiet places are, who I can go to if I need something and where other things that I need are located. I have developed relationships with several monks and other friendly and helpful Abbey personnel.

Some churches are adding retreats to their pastors' job descriptions, which is a great thing. If this isn't the case at your church, I encourage you to write a proposal to add retreats to your job description.

Pilgrimage. The pilgrimage is about the adventure of traveling to a spiritually meaningful place with Christ as your traveling companion. Every follower of Jesus is called to a life of pilgrimage, following a God on the move. Embarking on a pilgrimage is a way to physically and spiritually focus intensely on the lifelong metaphor of Christianity as a journey in the way of Jesus.

Pilgrimages are found throughout the Old and New Testaments. Abraham was called to journey with God, and by faith he traveled to the land of promise. The Psalms pronounce pilgrims as blessed: "Blessed are those whose strength is in you, who have set their hearts on pilgrimage" (Ps 84:5 NIV). Psalms 120—134 were written specifically to be sung while traveling to Zion and the temple. Jesus and his family, like most good Jewish families living in the second temple period, most likely made several pilgrimages annually to Jerusalem. The Scripture records a specific account of one such pilgrimage when Jesus, after being inadvertently left in Jerusalem by his parents, ended up confounding the scholars in the temple with his profound knowledge and insight.

Pilgrimage also played a key role throughout the life of the early church. Origen, a third-century church father, spoke of the passion that followers of Jesus had to walk in the "footsteps of Christ, of the Prophets and of the Apostles." Pilgrimages were common for the early church, continued through the middle ages, and are now becoming a more prominent spiritual practice for many. The most common pilgrimage of the church through the ages has been to visit the places mentioned in Scripture, especially Jerusalem and Bethlehem.

As a part of my rule of life I desire to make at least one pilgrimage each year. A pilgrimage once every three or five years may be more achievable. Resources are available for affordable pilgrimages in North America and abroad. Still, travel to the places where the events of Scripture occurred are usually the first destinations that come to mind, including Israel, Italy, Greece, Egypt, Jordan and Turkey.

Here are other pilgrimage ideas:

- Santiago de Compostela in northwestern Spain where James, the disciple of Jesus, is believed to be buried.

- Iona, an island off the west coast of Scotland, where the Celtic missionary Saint Columba built a monastery in the sixth century.

- Canterbury in England, where Thomas Becket, the Archbishop of Canterbury, was martyred. This pilgrimage site was popularized by Chaucer's *The Canterbury Tales*.

- Ireland, with many historic sites like Glendalough and Clonmacnois.

- Taizé, a prayer community in the south of France. Every week during the summer, thousands of young people spend a week in prayer at this unique place.

- Famous North American missions like San Juan Capistrano along the coast of California, or the great cathedrals in New York City.

- The Appalachian Trail, a peaceful Ozark River canoe trip, or camping in the Rocky Mountains.

Even something as simple as returning to the places of your childhood could be an amazing spiritual experience.

Body care. Body care is a very important issue within youth ministry. Adolescents are bombarded by erroneous messages about bodies. Our bodies are a gift from God, not a curse. We desperately need a theology of the body that correctly views bodies as a wonderful creation of God.

Our body is not just a thing that we use as a tool to be discarded for good when we die and go to heaven. We *are* bodies—embodied souls. Our great hope involves a bodily resurrection. Our bodies play a key role in our Christian formation. Our bodies enable us to serve, communicate and worship. Taking care of our bodies is an important spiritual practice. Paul, in his first epistle to the Corinthians, reminds them that their bodies belong to God, and they are therefore to glorify God with their bodies.

We are embodied souls. The fact that we are physical and spiritual beings cannot be separated. Being human means having bodies— bodies that aren't necessarily obstacles to our spirits. Our bodies are wonderful creations, not evil prisons that we hope to escape from one day. No doubt our bodies can be used for evil and can get in the way of our spiritual lives. Nevertheless, our bodies are good, made by God. We are called to be good stewards of this gift.

Our bodies are inseparably a part of our identity and our spiritual formation, so they are a major factor in our spiritual vitality. Many Christians misuse their bodies because they hold the attitude that their bodies aren't nearly as important as the spiritual part of them: *My body is just going to die anyway.* And yet, belief in a resurrection means that physical matter has a destiny.

It is Jesus' resurrected body that teaches us, perhaps more than any other image in Christianity, that bodies matter. In the resurrection narratives of the New Testament, Jesus insists on his body: "Look at my hands and my feet," he says in Luke's Gospel. "See that it is I myself. Touch me and see." Offering his hands and feet for inspection, Jesus gives his followers the foundation of the new vision that will be required of them as they strive to follow him when he is no longer walking and talking by their side. "Touch me," he says, "and see." Jesus offers his body as the lens through which the disciples must look if they—and we— are to respond to the world's needs with love.[2]

Orthodoxy (correct thinking) seamlessly integrated with *orthopraxis* (right practice) is essential for living in the way of Jesus. Incorporating this understanding into a rule of life means that we acknowledge the importance of our bodies in our Christian formation. We utilize our bodies in prayer practices. We develop liturgical practices that underscore the bodily enactment of our faith. We care for our body as a good creation of God through proper nutrition and physical exercise. We access discipline and training practices such as fasting and temperance to properly subjugate our bodies to the obedience of Christ.

God will make our bodies anew, not make us new bodies. A rule of life thus includes disciplines related to body care, such as exercise, nutrition and rest. Committing to an exercise routine helps us to be physically fit and serves as a way to practice mastery over our bodies. My wife and I love to run together. I also enjoy long runs and bike rides alone. These times provide not only great exercise but an excellent way to think, pray and meditate on Scripture. Some of my best ideas come when I'm running or biking.

We should be concerned about all the negative ramifications of being overweight. I know that many people have physical or genetic issues that lead to being overweight. However, a lot of our problems with weight control have to do with our eating habits. We should have limits to what kind of and how much fast food we eat. Likewise we should not fall into the quest to measure up to unrealistic body images presented in our society.

Sabbath rest affects the body along with the soul. I know some who have dancing as a part of their spiritual rule of life. Even though it is not a formal part of my rule of life I take note of how long it has been since I have had a good belly laugh because laughter is good medicine.

The bottom line—our bodies are the temple of the Holy Spirit, which means we need to seriously consider the role our body plays in the gospel. Maintaining spiritual practices for body care should be a part of your rule of life. This will help you to embrace a more holistic spirituality that rightly views the role our bodies play in our Christian formation.

Hospitality. Hospitality is the practice of entertaining and serving guests—strangers and friends. We need to be intentional about making space and time for others, discerning their needs and making efforts to meet them. It's a significant ingredient of community, and for some this is an important aspect of a rule of life.

Hospitality is recommended throughout Scripture, by command and example.

> Be hospitable to one another without complaining. Like good stewards of the manifold grace of God, serve one another with whatever gift each of you has received. . . . Whoever serves must do so with the strength that God supplies, so that God may be glorified in all things through Jesus Christ. (1 Pet 4:9-11)

When we are hospitable, we don't focused solely on our friends; we also extend ourselves to the marginalized, "the least of these."

Examination of conscience. The examination of conscience (discussed in more detail in the chapter on prayer practices) enables us to focus, listen and discern the positive and passionate things of God and the working of the Holy Spirit that is going on within us (consolation) along with acknowledging the times when we seem to be furthest away from the love of God (desolation).

This spiritual practice as a part of your rule of life could be one you do on a daily, weekly, monthly or annual basis. Examination of conscience is a good practice to combine with other parts of your rule of life. For example, you might include a statement like, "I will engage in an examination of conscience for an extended period of time twice a year when I go on my spiritual retreat," or "I will practice examination of conscience, once a month during a sabbath rest."

Focal points. Focal points are intentionally placed art, jewelry, pictures, tokens or other physical objects that draw our attention to God or remind us of a spiritual truth. This isn't typically on a list of spiritual practices, but I add these to the options for a rule of life because they're meaningful to me.

As I sit in my office, I see my icon of *Saint Menas with Christ,* which I refer to as *Traveling Companions* because it reminds me that the spiritual life is not an individual endeavor. I see a painting of Jerusalem's Western Wall, which reminds me of the passion of prayer and of my many pilgrimages to Jerusalem.

At home I have a crucifix on my bedside table to remind me every morning that I have a Savior and that he calls me to pick up my cross, deny myself and follow him. We have a mezuzah—a parchment containing the text of Joshua 24:15—rolled up in a case and placed on the frame of our front door. I have a communion set from Taizé sitting on my desk at the office.

I have an auditory focal point too. Every time I hear a bell ring, it reminds me of the call to prayer and other spiritually uplifting things I've associated with bells.

Confession. Confession is not simply the recognition of a mistake. Confession is the acceptance of responsibility for our behavior and attitudes that do not conform to the ways of God. Confession is part of the calling of God on our life to repent. Confession has both inward ramifications—self-discovery, cleansing, honesty and responsibility—and outward ramifications—reconciliation, authenticity and relationship building. Confession has private and public components.

The Old Testament has many exhortations to confess. The New Testament likewise calls for confession: "Therefore confess your sins to one another, and pray for one another, so that you may be healed" (Jas 5:16).

Confession as a public act varies depending on tradition, denomination and congregation. Public confession is usually expressed in a liturgical manner such as reciting the Lord's Prayer ("Forgive our sins as we forgive those who sin against us") or, psalms or litanies of confession and repentance. Private confession occurs somewhere on the continuum between formal (confession to a priest) and informal (perhaps spontaneous conversation with a friend). Within the evangelical tradition, confession usually occurs between two friends who have a trust relationship with each other. Sometimes this is referred to as holding each other accountable.

Our confession and repentance is not only an obedient response to God but also a relational response toward others. For me, the ultimate act of confession happens every time I partake of the Eucharist. I examine my life and confess sin to Christ as I engage in this sacrament with the rest of my community. Partaking of the Eucharist is a solemn remembrance of the grace and forgiveness provided to me along with a celebration of the eschaton—our future gathering at the banquet table of God.

Networking. One of the greatest joys I have had in youth ministry over the last decade has been the networking and partnering relationships I have shared with other youth workers. I have found the movement out of a sectarian mindset to a broad-based, ecumenical connectivity (mainline, evangelical, Orthodox, Catholic) to be fulfilling and life-giving.

Too many youth workers are devoid of adult relationships. Not having significant adult friendships and networks is dangerous, as Kenda Creasy Dean writes:

> No wonder people who pastor youth stress out, wear out, and burn out faster than people in almost any other form of ministry. Our root systems are in terrible shape. A Carnegie Council on Adolescent Development study identified a "lack of networking" as one of the most devastating problems facing religious youth workers.
>
> The absence of these networks reinforces the image of youth ministry as an alienated, isolated profession. Most of us do not know what the church across the street (much less around the world) is doing with youth, so we reinvent the wheel every day. We are neither connected to Jesus Christ nor to each other in ways that adequately feed our souls or the souls of young people.[3]

As a part of my rule of life, I have placed a high value on networking and ecumenical dialogue. I've learned much about youth ministry and life by seeking these meaningful relationships. I have also mentored other youth workers. The more clearly I see the diversity of the body of Christ in all its splendid varieties, the more I am enriched and inspired. Through these relationships I am blessed and able to glimpse the larger picture of God at work in the world.

Youth ministry is not easy even with wonderful networks and significant relationships strengthening you. I say presence-centered youth ministry, even more than other aspects of Christian ministry, is dependent on a strong community of relationships. For the health of your own soul and the integrity of your life, seek authentic relationships with other adults and youth workers.

A RULE OF LIFE FOR YOUTH GROUPS

Consider developing a rule of life for your youth group as well. It can be a powerful way to connect your youth to the spiritual practices we've dealt with in this book and address other issues facing them:

- the desire to connect to the early church and tradition
- the embodiment of their faith
- the challenge and cost of being a disciple of Jesus
- the connection between personal faith and a faith community
- the tangible expression of faith within a local community
- the emphasis on being a servant and living out faith
- the embrace of family spiritual heirlooms
- the emphasis on classic Christian formation
- the deemphasizing of activities that don't lead to genuine transformation

I'm not surprised if your first response is, "This won't work" or "He obviously doesn't have my kids in mind when he makes this suggestion." I only ask you to not dismiss the idea of creating a youth ministry rule of life too quickly.

Just as with a personal rule of life, developing one for your youth

> Lead a life worthy of the calling to which you have been called, with all humility and gentleness, with patience, bearing with one another in love, making every effort to maintain the unity of the Spirit in the bond of peace. There is one body and one Spirit, just as you were called to the one hope of your calling, one Lord, one faith, one baptism, one God and Father of all, who is above all and through all and in all.
>
> **EPHESIANS 4:1-6**

ministry should start out simple and develop as your kids mature. An entire youth group or a discipleship group within the larger youth group may wish to develop a rule of life; the youth involved should take part in creating the rule, crafting it broadly enough that individuals can develop their own personal rule of life under the umbrella of the youth group. For instance, "Our youth group will be a praying youth group" is broad enough to get started. The individual youth can develop more specificity for their personal rules. It can also be developed into a more specific plan later.

You cannot develop or learn to live by a rule of life in a short time. Athletes don't excel in their sport spontaneously, nor do musicians pick up an instrument and master it in a day. Seeing young people become authentic and passionate followers of Jesus doesn't happen quickly either. Christian formation takes time, a lifetime. But training is required, and teaching youth how to live by a rule of life is important.

We need to find the right tension between calling our youth to a challenging and faith-stretching place and burdening them with unhealthy expectations that aren't realistic. This is where creating environments of transformation is so important. We teach and guide them. We nurture opportunities for them to encounter the presence of the Holy Spirit.

When a youth worker has the opportunity to see the youth engage passionately in prayer, meditation, Scripture and worship in powerful ways, we find nothing more fulfilling. It's essential for your youth to be involved in the development of a rule of life in a way that helps them own it. Besides those mentioned in the previous chapter, you may want to consider some additional values and practices for your youth group's rule of life.

The arts. Young people today are interested in rediscovering the role of the arts in the life of the church. George Gallup Jr. draws attention to the importance of reclaiming the role of artistic expression in worship, ministry and witness:

> People are interested in experiences that engage all their senses. Historically the church often was patron to great pieces of music and art, from Bach chorales to the Sistine Chapel. Church leaders need to discover new ways in which the church in the twenty-first century can encourage artistic expression and the use of the arts to express faith, worship, to witness to what we know and believe. How can the church encourage and sponsor new forms of poetry, music, mime, drama, cinema, theater?[4]

One of the ways we can encourage engaging in the arts is to place a high value on them and break down the secular-sacred dichotomy. A youth group's rule of life could say something like, "We will express the talents of our group to create art in all forms for the glory of God and for the edification of each other and our community."

Technology. Technology and new media communication is another area you may want to incorporate into your youth group's rule of life. Technology is definitely changing our lives and our lifestyles and is creating many new and powerful ways to communicate, learn and express creativity.

Play. Some could draw a conclusion that there is no room for fun in a rule of life and no space for play or events or programs. "After all, this is all about presence-centered youth ministry where all we do is pray, meditate on Scripture, seek solitude and so on." Not true! Everyone likes to have fun and enjoy life. We need a theology of play not only for youth ministry but for the entire church to realize that we can have fun to the glory of God.

Celebration. Christians, of all people, should be a celebratory people. Including celebration in a rule of life could mean celebrating religious seasons of the church, such as Lent and Advent. The end of Lent can be a celebration connected to the resurrection of the Son of God. Advent leads to the celebration of the incarnation. Christians should be great party people.

Service and social justice. Being outward-focused and engaging in service is an important part of an adolescent's Christian formation. One of the first abstract concepts a child proclaims is, "That's not fair!" A desire for justice is a natural response of human beings. This desire only grows when we dwell in the presence of God. One of the truly significant things that emerges from presence-centered youth ministry is a passion to engage in works of mercy and justice. This is a natural—or maybe supernatural—progression from the fruit of prayer, worship and meditating on Scripture.

Seeing the acts of mercy and social justice that adolescents are engaging in has been one of the most fulfilling aspects of my ministry. It's contagious. And this is as it should be. The message of Jesus Christ has always been revolutionary. Jesus never played it safe, and adolescent passion is drawn to that kind of spirituality.

I considered calling this chapter "A Rule of Life for People Who Don't Like Rules" because, as I stated earlier, the word *rule* has such a grating effect on most of us. A rule of life fulfills a good purpose— it reminds us that we are not the center of the cosmos. God is. A rule of life celebrates our joyful commitment to Jesus Christ and our desire to be habituated in the way of Jesus. A rule of life helps us become full participants in God's inbreaking kingdom.

The last thing we want for our rule of life is for a legalistic mentality to develop, or the concept that our rule of life gets us to heaven. Too many churches develop a "this is the way we do it here" mentality that operates as a rule of life, but with little to do with living in the way of Jesus. This kind of rule of life will inspire very few to pick up a cross.

On the other hand, viewing a rule of life as a means of participating with our awesome God in the world is compelling, exciting and dangerous enough to totally captivate many with a passion to lay down their life.

> Then I saw a new heaven and a new earth; for the first heaven and the first earth had passed away, and the sea was no more. And I saw the holy city, the new Jerusalem, coming down out of heaven from God, prepared as a bride adorned for her husband. And I heard a loud voice from the throne saying,
>
> "See, the home of God is among mortals. He will dwell with them as their God; they will be his peoples, and God himself will be with them; he will wipe every tear from their eyes. Death will be no more; mourning and crying and pain will be no more, for the first things have passed away."
>
> And the one who was seated on the throne said, "See, I am making all things new." Also he said, "Write this, for these words are trustworthy and true." Then he said to me, "It is done! I am the Alpha and the Omega, the beginning and the end. To the thirsty I will give water as a gift from the spring of the water of life. Those who conquer will inherit these things, and I will be their God and they will be my children." (Rev 21:1-7)

To colabor with God for the renewal of all things is an awesome and gripping vision—a vision I believe can capture not only our hearts but also the imagination and passion of the young people we work with.

ELEVEN

The Art of the Long View

One of my favorite cathedrals in North America is one of the world's greatest: Saint John the Divine in New York City. It was first conceived in the 1820s. The ground-breaking ceremony didn't happen for another six decades. Today, though this cathedral is magnificent, it is only two-thirds complete. The date of completion is projected to be at least a hundred years from now. When finally finished, it will be the second largest religious structure in the world. At least three hundred years will have passed from the time it was conceived until it will be finished.

Three hundred years is relatively quick compared to many of the great cathedrals built during the medieval period. Cathedrals are built by people who understand the art of the long view.

The art of the long view is something that we must embrace if we are going to engage in the Christian formation that we have been examining in this book. We live in an age in which we want instantaneous results. Yet this impatient expectancy for outcomes doesn't seem to match up well with the overarching narrative of Scripture. God waited forty years for Moses to mature in the desert. Jesus gives us a lifetime to work on "getting it." If Jesus is that graceful with us, we can be equally gracious and patient with the young people we work with.

How many young people come to our events and programs is not the most important way to evaluate how our ministry is doing. Forming Christians who have godly character and a passion for Christ doesn't happen overnight. We should be thinking about where our young people will be in their life with God not only next week, but also ten or forty years from now. Cutting corners to get immediate spiritual results with our youth will rarely last. Presence-centered youth ministry is about helping youth understand that they aren't defined by what they accomplish but only by who they are in Jesus Christ. This takes time. This takes commitment to a lifelong journey of faithfully seeking the face of God and living in the way of Jesus.

Learning to practice the presence of God in their lives will sustain adolescents in their journey long after they are gone from the youth group. Equipping them with the skills to hear the Holy Spirit speak through Scripture, to care for their souls and to commit to a community of people who are on the same journey—are essential for long-term faithfulness in the pursuit of Christ.

A spiritual journey means moving step by step into new territory utterly dependent upon the Holy Spirit. We don't have it all figured out. We don't have all the answers. We don't always know which way to turn. We often feel lost. We experience ups and downs, victories and set backs, sorrows and joy, understanding and confusion, faith and doubt. This is the norm for a life well lived.

THE McDONALDIZATION OF CHRISTIANITY

Unfortunately, too many youth grow up hearing that all they need to do is say yes to God and they will have a wonderful and happy life. It doesn't take long for young people to discover the shallowness of this mentality. They come to agree with Thomas Merton who said, "If you find God with great ease, perhaps it is not God that you have found."

Too often we present a spirituality that resembles our obsession with instantaneous gratification and results. Many have spoken of this tendency as the McDonaldization of Christianity. There is an expectation for our Christian formation to return exactly what we want as quickly as it takes to announce our order through a microphone and pull up to the drive-through window to receive our request. Mike Yaconelli confronts this "hurried discipleship" as contrary to Jesus' intent:

> Jesus' program of discipleship was simple: hang out with the disciples; let them see you at your best and worst; spend lots of time alone; teach truths none of your disciples can grasp at the moment; avoid crowds; go slowly; spend hours in solitude; don't worry about opposition; ignore criticism; and don't expect immediate results.
>
> Jesus knew hurried disciples become ex-disciples. Modern youth ministry needs to understand our mission: planting, watering and waiting . . . in other words, unhurried discipleship. Jesus knew, and so should we, that discipleship lasts a lifetime.[1]

JOURNEY FOR A LIFETIME

When we expect immediate results of faith development among our youth, we hijack a process that's unpredictable. We are called to youth ministry to be spiritual guides for the youth we experience life with. Whether we have a deep walk with Christ or a shallow faith we are guiding youth spiritually, either in a healthy or a dysfunctional manner.

The most important thing we bring to our youth ministry is a heart seeking the face of God and a life that is truly lived in God's presence. My life with Christ has been strengthened and challenged by being around mentors and friends who have a contagious and vibrant faith in Jesus. To see someone who is filled with passion for God and yet is authentic enough to let me see their struggles, doubts and weaknesses gives me hope and joy for the journey that I'm on.

One of the things I say constantly in light of spending more than thirty years in youth ministry is that I refuse to grow up. What I am really saying is that I will not abandon my overflowing passion for life. I want to continue to be childlike in my fascination with a life that will never run out of new discoveries and opportunities. My life is consumed with God. I am obsessed with knowing and seeking Jesus.

When every aspect of our lives is lived out enmeshed with the rhythm of God at work in the world even the mundane and simple things of life explode with meaning. As Frederick Buechner puts it,

> There is no event so commonplace but that God is present in it, always hiddenly, always leaving you to recognize him or not to recognize him, but all the more fascinatingly because of that, all the more compellingly and hauntingly.[2]

A conversation with a friend becomes a time of enlightenment. A cup of coffee turns into a time of contemplation. A shared meal becomes a sacrament. A movie leads to new awareness. A song lifts us into the heavenlies. A poem inspires us to new vistas of possibilities. A round of laughter leads to healing. A nap gives new perspective on life. A gentle breeze reminds us that the whole world is filled with the presence of God. These and thousands upon thousands of moments are part of what Jesus promised when he came to give us life to the full.

I want to see adolescents transformed by youth workers who live out of a presence-centered life. That means embracing the art of the long view, knowing it might take a while for the youth to get it. In reality, though, who among us isn't still trying to get it? I want young people to discover the joy of Jesus in all of life, from major events to the simplest details.

This lifelong journey with Christ is not simple, but neither is it overwhelming. Jesus comes to us with life abundantly. The heart of being a youth worker as a spiritual guide leading a presence-centered youth ministry is found in Matthew 11:28-30:

> Come to me, all you that are weary and are carrying heavy burdens, and I will give you rest. Take my yoke upon you, and learn from me; for I am gentle and humble in heart, and you will find rest for your souls. For my yoke is easy, and my burden is light.

We must sit at the feet of the master to learn the way of Jesus. We must become an apprentice to our Lord and Savior. Come to and learn from Jesus Christ.

Conclusion

Where Are You Staying?

Looking back, it was a major crossroad in my life. I needed to get away and hear from God. During my week away with Jesus I focused on John 1:35-39 (NIV):

> The next day John was there again with two of his disciples. When he saw Jesus passing by, he said, "Look, the Lamb of God!"
>
> When the two disciples heard him say this, they followed Jesus. Turning around, Jesus saw them following and asked, "What do you want?"
>
> They said, "Rabbi" (which means Teacher), "where are you staying?"
>
> "Come," he replied, "and you will see."
>
> So they went and saw where he was staying, and spent that day with him.

I read this text practicing lectio divina several times a day. I used phrases from it to center myself. I meditated, contemplated and prayed with this amazing text. Four days into my retreat I climbed up the side of a mountain, rolled out a blanket and used the Ignatian prayer exercise of imaginative prayer to interact with the words.

I determined to imagine and pray through this text in real time. I didn't have to spend a lot of time imagining the geography, the smells, the sounds, because I have been to Israel twenty times, so I know approximately where this event took place. I know what the Jordan River looks like near the Dead Sea, close to Jericho. I know what the weather is like, how thick the vegetation is near the meandering banks of the Jordan River. I was able to fixate on what may have happened when Jesus came over the bank and headed toward John the Baptist and his delegation.

I imagined myself sitting around John's breakfast fire with his disciples, listening as his disciples began to discuss the plans for another day of baptizing. I imagined the personalities of these people who would follow the unconventional "baptizer" into this desolate area. And then, Jesus came through the thick vegetation over the bank toward John's camp next to the Jordan River. John stopped midsentence and said, "Look, the Lamb of God!" I saw John and his cousin Jesus embrace.

Jesus and the few who were with him joined us around the fire. I imagined what it would have been like to hear stories of Jesus and John's boyhood visits to each other's families. I heard laughter along with serious discussions of God and his coming kingdom.

And then Jesus abruptly rose to leave. They said their goodbyes and Jesus and his few followers left. The two disciples of John followed Jesus and I imagined myself right behind them, going along to see what would happen. We hit a trail through the thicket heading into the desert. As we came into a clearing Jesus turned around, seeing the two disciples of John following him.

What happened next is just as real to me as if I was actually there in the text. I have shared this experience about a dozen and a half times, never without tears because of how deeply this affected me, even writing this now is very emotional.

When Jesus turned around, the two disciples of John whom I was following parted like the Red Sea and Jesus came right up to me, face to face. Jesus looked past my eyes into my heart and soul:

"Mike, what do you want?"

I fell at the feet of Jesus and wept, pouring my heart out, praying, confessing, and in the end my answer was the same as John's disciples. "Where are you staying? Because that is right where I want to be. I want you Jesus. I want to remain with you. To go where you go, to learn from you, to love you, to be with you."

For one year after that experience I meditated every day on this text. I have often used imaginative prayer since that experience. Many times the Holy Spirit has met me and spoken to me, though never with the intensity that I experienced God that day on the side of a mountain. But that day changed me profoundly and is something I will have for the rest of my life, for Jesus said, "Come, and you will see."[1]

Epilogue

In the introduction I shared the story of Tylor. He knew that life meant to passionately yet humbly pursue the presence of God and be transformed by sitting at the feet of Jesus. He wasn't flashy, but he had taken seriously a calling issued two thousand years ago by Jesus of Nazareth: "If any want to become my followers, let them deny themselves and take up their cross daily and follow me. For those who want to save their life will lose it, and those who lose their life for my sake will save it" (Lk 9:23-24).

In closing, I want to share another chapter of Tylor's life. A year after Tylor's death, Brad tells his story:

> Since middle school I'd known him. He was the guy that would come up and spark a conversation just to meet you. Though Tylor and I never got the chance to become close, one thing I did understand from being around him. Tylor had a real connection with this friend of his named Jesus.
>
> I attended Tylor's vigil at Blue Springs South High School along with hundreds of others. Many were crying. But their tears looked like tears of joy. It seemed more of a celebration than a vigil. At the same time, the whole experience left me feel-

ing shattered. It shouldn't have because I wasn't that close to Tylor.

Later that night I couldn't sleep. I could sense God was trying to get my attention. I turned on the light and pulled out my old, rarely touched Bible. The mental and emotional battle of Tylor's death had worn me down. God was taking the opportunity to step in. That next weekend I went to church with my friend Drew. I felt like I belonged there. Slowly Jesus' promises and the redemption story started to sink in.

As I began to seriously reflect on my thoughts and emotions, some things were becoming clear. It was my lack of trust in God that had kept me from pursuing a better friendship with Tylor and with Tylor's friend, Jesus. And that night at Tylor's vigil— my heart had been crying out for God's help and grace, but my "intellect" kept telling me that there was no way his God could be real.

It all came together on December 28. That was the day I put my trust in Jesus Christ. Looking back now, before Tylor's death, the Holy Spirit had been putting people in my life that quietly caused me to question myself. At the same time, they accepted me no matter what I said I believed or didn't believe. They were planting seeds in my life. And what God did for me upon Tylor's death was the budding of those seeds.

Tylor's life, his actions, his words, just shouted God: love the Lord your God with all your heart, soul, and strength. This is what Tylor did and did earnestly. It's a heart that we should all take from him, we should all follow God that hard.

Notes

Introduction
[1]Thomas Merton, quoted in Leonard Sweet, *AquaChurch* (Loveland, Colo.: Group, 1999).

Chapter 1: Three Decades of Youth Ministry
[1]Going to the prom—dancing—was a big issue in many youth groups in the 1970s, and it still is for some today.

[2]During this time I was drawn to Mike Yaconelli, the founder of Youth Specialties, who was full of passion for God, for youth workers, for life, for truth and for honesty. In the years that followed I had many significant encounters with him. These encounters—along with his articles, books and messages—profoundly shaped me.

[3]Dallas Willard's book *Divine Conspiracy* (San Francisco: HarperSanFrancisco, 1998) was an enormous influence on my spiritual life.

Chapter 2: Dysfunctional Evangelical Youth Ministry
[1]This statistic was reported by Southern Baptist Council on Family Life to the 2002 Annual Meeting of the Southern Baptist Convention. It is also a part of the Christian Education Resolution for the Southern Baptist Convention, June 2004 <www/exodusmandate.org/art_christian-education-resolution-sbc.htm>. Statistics similar to this have surfaced in other denominational circles. Ironically, it seems that those who cite these statistics most often are using them to declare war on the culture and entrench more deeply in their resistance to change, unaware that this mentality may be the very thing driving so many youth away from the church.

[2]Robert E. Webber, "What Younger Evangelicals Want—and Are Getting!" interview on Homiletics Online, <www.homileticsonline.com/subscriber/interviews/webber.asp>.

[3]Tony Campolo, National Pastors Conference, San Diego, spring 2002.

[4]"Surprisingly Few Adults Outside of Christianity Have Positive Views of Christians," *Barna Update,* December 3, 2002.

[5]Michael Spencer, "Why Do They Hate Us?" <www.internetmonk.com/articles/H/hateus.html> (no longer available). Christians are disliked for many reasons that have nothing to do with the gospel.

[6]Peter C. Glover, "Does It Matter What They Think?" <www.evangelical-times.org/articles/Oct03/oct03a11.htm> June 14, 2005.

[7]D. G. Hart, *Deconstructing Evangelicalism* (Grand Rapids: Baker Academic, 2004), p. 19.

[8]Theologian Stanley Hauerwas believes the message of Jesus Christ is radical and calls for followers of Jesus to be resident aliens, not fully connected to any political system but embracing instead God's kingdom agenda. We will be a peculiar people who may be misunderstood by the world around us, but may it be for the right reasons mentioned in Scripture, not because we're idiots. The youth of today are eager to embrace the agenda of God's kingdom when it explores more categories than simply Republican or Democrat, liberal or conservative.

[9]Hart, *Deconstructing Evangelicalism,* p. 109.

[10]Ibid., p. 82.

[11]Tom Sine, *Mustard Seed Versus McWorld* (Grand Rapids: Baker, 1999), p. 41.

[12]Spencer, "Why Do They?"

[13]Miroslav Volf discusses these issues in the introduction of *After Our Likeness: The Church as the Image of Trinity* (Grand Rapids: Eerdmans, 1998). The introduction alone is worth the price of the book.

Chapter 3: A Convergence of Fronts

[1]Henry H. Knight III, *A Future for Truth: Evangelical Theology in a Postmodern World* (Nashville: Abingdon, 1997), p. 167.

[2]Christian Smith and Melinda Lundquist Denton, *Soul Searching: The Religious and Spiritual Lives of American Teenagers* (Oxford: Oxford University Press, 2005), pp. 162-63.

Chapter 4: A New Kind of Youth Worker

[1]Brennan Manning, *Signature of Jesus* (Old Tappan, N.J.: Chosen, 1988), p. 38.

[2]Robert E. Webber, "What Younger Evangelicals Want—and Are Getting!" interview on Homiletics Online <www.homileticsonline.com/subscriber/interviews/webber.asp>.

[3]Manning, *Signature of Jesus,* p. 73.

[4]Kenda Creasy Dean, *Practicing Passion: Youth and the Quest for a Passionate Church* (Grand Rapids: Eerdmans, 2004), p. 48.

[5]Colleen Carroll, *The New Faithful: Why Young Adults are Embracing Christian Orthodoxy* (Chicago: Loyola Press, 2002), p. 62.

Chapter 5: The Youth Worker as Spiritual Guide
[1]Brother Lawrence, *The Practice of the Presence of God*, trans. Robert J. Edmonson (Brewster, Mass.: Paraclete, 1985), p. 103
[2]Ibid., p. 48.
[3]Robert Webber, *The Younger Evangelicals* (Grand Rapids: Baker, 2002), pp. 189-90.
[4]Paul Gauche, "The Cool Church," *Group Magazine,* May/June 2001, p. 37.
[5]Richard John Neuhaus, quoted in Eddie Gibbs, *ChurchNext* (Downers Grove, Ill.: InterVarsity Press, 2000), p. 116.
[6]I don't remember where I first heard this story, but I've remembered it because I think the man's assessment is quite accurate.
[7]Brennan Manning, *Signature of Jesus* (Old Tappan, N.J.: Chosen, 1988), p. 124.
[8]Gibbs, *ChurchNext*, pp. 40-41.
[9]Ibid., p. 130.
[10]Ibid., pp. 129-30.
[11]Gordon Mursell, ed., *The Story of Christian Spirituality: Two Thousand Years, from East to West* (Minneapolis: Fortress Press, 2001), p. 162.

Chapter 6: Trusting the Holy Spirit with Your Ministry
[1]A. W. Tozer, *The Pursuit of God* (Camp Hill, Penn.: Christian Publications, 1993), p. 37.

Chapter 7: Connecting Youth to the Story of God
[1]G. K. Chesterton, *Orthodoxy* (New York: John Lane, 1908), p. 85.
[2]D. G. Hart, *Deconstructing Evangelicalism* (Grand Rapids: Baker Academic, 2004), p. 179.
[3]Michael Horton, *We Believe* (Nashville: Word, 1998), pp. 6-8.
[4]The closest tradition to nonliturgical are Quakers who worship in silence waiting for someone to speak to the rest of the congregation as led by the Holy Spirit.
[5]Ronald E. Eggert, comp., *Tozer on Leadership* (Harrisburg, Penn.: Wingspread, 2001).
[6]Eddie Gibbs, *ChurchNext* (Downers Grove, Ill.: InterVarsity Press, 2000), p. 133.
[7]Henri J. M. Nouwen, Donald P. McNeill and Douglas A. Morrison, *Compassion: A Reflection on the Christian Life* (New York: Image/Doubleday, 1982), pp. 90-91.

Chapter 8: Prayer Practices for Presence-Centered Youth Ministry
[1]Ignatius of Loyola, *The Spiritual Exercises,* trans. Pierre Wolff (Liguori, Mo.:Liguori/

Triumph, 1997), 316 (Third Rule).

[2]Ignatius *Spiritual Exercises* 317 (Fourth Rule).

[3]Ignatius *Spiritual Exercises* 322 (Ninth Rule), my paraphrase.

[4]Chotkis like mine aren't cheap because they're intricate and handmade. You can find chotkis online by visiting <www.easternchristian.com>.

[5]Tertullian *De Corona* 30.

[6]"Why Do Lutherans Make the Sign of the Cross?" Evangelical Lutheran Church of America, January 2003 <www.elca.org/dcm/worship/faq/liturgy/sign_of_cross.html>.

[7]Henri J. M. Nouwen, *Behold the Beauty of the Lord: Praying with Icons* (Notre Dame, Ind.: Ave Maria, 1987), pp. 12-14.

[8]Phyllis Tickle, *The Divine Hours* (New York: Doubleday, 2000), pp. ix-x.

Chapter 9: Using Scripture in Presence-Centered Youth Ministry

[1]Henry H. Knight III, *A Future for Truth: Evangelical Theology in a Postmodern World* (Nashville: Abingdon, 1997), p. 51.

[2]George Gallup Jr. and Timothy Jones, *The Next American Spirituality: Finding God in the Twenty-First Century* (Colorado Springs: Chariot Victor, 2000), p. 149.

[3]Richard Hays, lecture at Nazarene Theological Seminary (Kansas City, Missouri), February 25, 2005.

[4]Gallup and Jones, *Next American Spirituality*, p. 149.

[5]Alister McGrath, *A Passion for Truth* (Downers Grove, Ill.: InterVarsity Press, 1996), p. 107.

[6]Roger Young, dir., *Jesus* (CBS, 1999).

[7]Eugene Peterson, *Take and Read: Spiritual Reading: An Annotated List* (Grand Rapids: Eerdmans, 1996), pp. ix-x.

[8]Saint Jerome, quoted in Mario Masini, *Lectio Divina,* trans. Edmund C. Lane (New York: Alba House, 1998), p. 83.

Chapter 10: A Rule of Life

[1]A lot of resources are available to help you develop your journaling. Visit <www.journalinglife.com>, <www.christian.livejournal.com> or <www.allaboutgod.com/journaling.htm> for good ideas and other resources.

[2]Stephanie Paulsell, in *Practicing Our Faith,* ed. Dorothy Bass (San Francisco: Jossey-Bass, 1997), p. 26.

[3]Kenda Creasy Dean and Ron Foster, *The Godbearing Life* (Nashville: Upper Room, 1998), p. 43.

[4]George Gallup Jr. and Timothy Jones, *The Next American Spirituality: Finding God in the Twenty-First Century* (Colorado Springs: Chariot Victor, 2000), p. 147.

Chapter 11: The Art of the Long View

[1]Mike Yaconelli, "Hurried Discipleship," *YouthWorker Journal*, January/February 2001.

[2]Frederick Buechner, *Listening to Your Life* (San Francisco: HarperSanFrancisco, 1992), p. 2.

Conclusion: Where Are You Staying?

[1]Originally published in Tony Jones, *The Sacred Way: Spiritual Practices for Everyday Life* (Grand Rapids: Zondervan, 2004), pp. 77-79. Reprinted courtesy of Zondervan.